Subculture

The Fragmentation of the Social

Chris Jenks

SAGE Publications
London • Thousand Oaks • New Delhi

SAGE Publications Ltd
1 Oliver's Yard
55 City Road
London EC1Y 1SP

SAGE Publications Inc
2455 Teller Road
Thousand Oaks, California 91320

SAGE Publications India Pvt Ltd
B-42 Panchsheel Enclave
Post Box 4109
New Delhi – 110 017

British Library Cataloguing in Publication data

A catalogue record for this book is available from the British Library

ISBN 0 7619 5370 1
ISBN 0 7619 5471 X

Library of Congress Control Number Available

Printed and bound in Great Britain by Athenaeum Press, Gateshead

Contents

For Barbara

About the Author

Chris Jenks is Professor of Sociology and Pro-Vice-Chancellor at Brunel University. His previous books include *Rationality, Education and the Social Organization of Knowledge* (Routledge, 1976), *Worlds Apart: Readings for a Sociology of Education* (with J. Beck, N. Keddie and M. Young) (Collier-Macmillan, 1977), *Toward a Sociology of Education* (with J. Beck, N. Keddie and M. Young) (Transaction, 1977); *The Sociology of Childhood* (Batsford, 1982); *Culture* (Routledge, 1993); *Cultural Reproduction* (Routledge, 1993); *Visual Culture* (Routledge, 1995); *Childhood* (Routledge, 1996); *Theorizing Childhood* (with A. James and A. Prout) (Polity, 1998); *Core Sociological Dichotomies* (Sage, 1998); *Images of Community: Durkheim, Social Systems and the Sociology of Art* (with J.A. Smith) (Ashgate, 2000); *Aspects of Urban Culture* (Sinica, 2001); *Culture: Critical Concepts*, 4 vols (Routledge, 2002); *Transgression* (Routledge, 2003); *Urban Culture*, 4 vols (Routledge, 2004); and *Qualitative Complexity* (with J.A. Smith) (Routledge, 2004). He is interested in sociological theory; post-structuralism and heterology; childhood; cultural theory; visual and urban culture; and extremes of behaviour.

Preface

This book has quite a long history, indeed, considerably longer than it took to write. Back in 1995 when I had just completed my themed trilogy on *Cultural Reproduction*, *Culture* and *Visual Culture*, my friend, commissioning editor and taskmaster, Chris Rojek, noticed that I appeared to have a small space in my life where I might relax. Abhorring, as he does, any signs of under-achievement, lethargy or even quietude, he came up with a proposal. Perhaps Hebdige's (1979) blockbuster *Subculture: The Meaning of Style* was showing signs of age; the various subcultures to which it referred were no longer current, they were becoming trace elements in popular culture's volatile memory. New communities, interest groups, scenes, assemblies, cults, fashions and style clusters were emerging, all of which might be formulated through the concept of subculture. Here was the niche for a new book and we talked through various possibilities ranging from the virtual associations of Internet chat rooms to the dark horrors of paedophile rings. An interesting prospect was emerging but I was not wholly convinced. My internal conversation about the possible work was complex and contradictory and overwhelmed my initial enthusiasm. It ran something like this: by virtue of having become a long-term inmate at Goldsmiths College I have worked with many of the ex-Birmingham CCCS scholars, including Paul Gilroy, Angela McRobbie, Dave Morely, Valerie Walkerdine, Richard Hoggart, Stuart Hall and, of course, Dick Hebdige. Now I get on extremely well with Dick but, much as I admired the orchid beauty of his mind, I had no desire to complete, replicate, stalk, shadow or sequel his project. Beyond that, the idea of creating a kind of 'Subculture Mark II' had a kind of greedy Hollywood excess about it.

Compounding these thoughts was the knowledge that Dick himself had felt that the concept had become pretty much exhausted and although I had, through the years, got around a bit in my various attempts to explain the social world, the idea of a 'subculture' had never been part of my analytic toolbox, nor had it ever held much appeal as a device. To me, the concept subculture had always seemed rather insular, parochial, a way of accounting for social action free from the constraints of collective structural life and, frankly, in its more modern iterations, subculture had become rather 'laddish'. There were other factors to consider: I was genuinely interested in exploring the dynamics of some of the groupings that we had considered as part of the new work but on a scale slightly in excess of a chapter each, so there was a danger of either glossing or over-condensing the substantive content.

Nevertheless there remained the idea of a 'subculture' and it was clear that although not of my own preference, this was an idea that had exercised considerable currency across sociology and cultural studies and one that seemed to have appeal to students. Although many regard the history of ideas as the 'trivial pursuits' end of intellectual work, I (perhaps only in common with Melvin Bragg) regard it as quite fascinating and instructive. So I began the book after a long delay during which time I had completed many more projects. The book was to be about the idea of subculture and not an account of a new collection of subcultures. This was exciting and provided the impetus to write, added to which was the certainty that the concept did not emerge in the 1970s because of the Birmingham people's desire to articulate working-class exclusion, interruption and resistance. I had encountered the concept well before that through my various paradoxical dalliances with Talcott Parsons, the Chicago School and criminology. Thus, I had a sense of lineage and a potential archaeology, I was engaged.

The book has emerged as an appraisal but also a sustained critique. I trust it will be of use to those who employ the concept of subculture in their research and also to commentators within our discipline. It should certainly appeal to students who, as ever, are attempting to put some of the many and complicated ideas that emerge from sociology into some kind of order.

Chris Jenks
Brunel University

ONE Mapping the Concept

The dividing line between 'a culture' and 'subculture' or 'cultural variant' has not yet been firmly staked out. (Kluckhohn and Kelley, 1962: 67)

Introduction

At the beginning of the twentieth century there occurred a remarkable series of developments in the philosophy of the human sciences that has come to be known as the 'linguistic turn'. Essentially, thinkers stopped regarding language as a neutral vehicle for the transmission of information or even simply as a behavioural form peculiar to the human species. Instead, and probably inspired by Ferdinand de Saussure's *Course in General Linguistics* (1916), language moved to centre stage, it assumed the status of a powerful and wholly appropriate root metaphor for the understanding and explanation of human conduct. Grammar, competence and performance, and versions of deep and surface structure became the new and enduring meta-concepts for conveying a sense of what was fundamentally human but also what was essentially social. Although in a number of disciplines, including sociology, these developments were slow in making themselves felt, they are now deeply established in debates across the spectrum of social theory deriving from structuralism, post-structuralism, deconstructionism, discourse theory, socio-linguistics and the sociology of language.

Though never quite superseding these formative developments, a second 'turn' has nevertheless occurred in the human sciences which, far from supplementing the core of the sociological tradition, has potentially threatened to destabilize its central concerns, its moral purpose and its methodological rigour. This de-traditionalization has been facilitated, in part, by what Chaney (1994) first referred to as the 'cultural turn' which many feel has contributed to the descent into, or at least the first teetering steps on the rocky road towards the postmodern. Culture has always been an important concept for sociology and anthropology but always in relation to a theory of social structure. Today, we might suggest, the idea of culture has gone feral and has become a soft resource for the description of meaningful human action without having to accept the responsibility of causality. Previously culture could be accurately understood from within a four-fold typology (Jenks, 1993b):

1 It was a cerebral or certainly a cognitive category; it was part of a general state of mind and it carried with it the idea of perfection, a goal of or an aspiration for individual human achievement or emancipation.
2 It was a more embodied and collective category; it invoked a state of intellectual and even moral development within a society.
3 It was a descriptive and concrete category; culture named the collective body of arts and intellectual work within any society.
4 Culture was a social category; it implied the whole way of life of a people.

Now culture, as an idea, has been both hijacked and adapted by the particular political agenda of cultural studies into a device for displacing the 'social' as a source of explanation (O'Neill, 1995). What does this mean? Well, let's attempt to inventory that agenda. Here is a list of attributes deriving from Agger's (1992) formulation of cultural studies as critical theory:

1 Cultural studies operates with an expanded concept of culture. It rejects the assumptions behind the 'culture debate' and thus rejects the high/low culture binary or, indeed, any attempt to re-establish the grounds for any cultural stratification. It adheres more closely to the anthropological view of culture as being 'the whole way of life of a people', though it does not subscribe to the view of culture as a totality.
2 Following on from the above, cultural studies legitimates, justifies, celebrates and politicizes all aspects of popular culture. It regards popular culture as valuable in its own right and not a 'shadow phenomenon', nor simply a vehicle for ideological mystification.
3 The proponents of cultural studies, as representative of their age, recognize the socialization of their own identities through the processes of mass media and communication that they seek to understand.
4 Culture is not viewed in stasis, as fixed or as a closed system. Cultural studies regards culture as emergent, as dynamic and as continual renewal.

Culture is not a series of artefacts or frozen symbols but is rather a process.

5   Cultural studies is predicated upon conflict rather than order. It investigates, and anticipates, conflict, both at the level of face-to-face interaction but also, and more significantly, at the level of meaning. Culture cannot be viewed as a unifying principle, a source of shared understanding or a mechanism for legitimating the social bond.

6   Cultural studies is 'democratically' imperialistic. As all aspects of social life are now 'cultured', then no part of social life is excluded from its interests – opera, fashion, gangland violence, pub talk, shopping, horror films, and so on … they are no longer colonized, canonized or zoned around a central meaning system.

7   Cultural representations are viewed by cultural studies at all levels – inception, mediation and reception, or production, distribution and consumption.

8   Cultural studies is interdisciplinary. It acknowledges no disciplinary origin, it encourages work on the interface of disciplinary concerns and it acknowledges a shifting and sprightly muse.

9   Cultural studies rejects absolute values – it does what it wants.

Implicit here is a calculated commitment to a fragmentation of the concept of society and the moral and political framework within which it is a meaningful part.

This erosion or death of the social also figures as an acceptable part of contemporary rightist and centrist political ideologies, vaunting self-help, free will and the powers and responsibilities of the individual. So, for example, following the 15 years of Thatcher's anti-'social' rhetoric in the UK, the alternative 'New Labour' movement elects for a 'third way', combining both public and private sectors, but also produces health and education as private rather than public goods. And although arising from a different place, within the academy, postmodernism's critical imperative recommending the end of grand narratives is an invitation to dispense with the power/knowledge, truth and authority on which society, and, in many senses, the social bond, of yesterday were established. Furthermore, the multiple meanings on which the concept of culture is based, have both encouraged and enabled cultural studies to justify, legitimate, celebrate and politicize all aspects of popular culture, whether aesthetic, transgressive, transitory or even downright silly. At one extreme, cultural studies in its most liberal and populist iterations rejects ultimate values, as stated above, and, in most senses, dispenses with theory in favour of stylistics and method in favour of insight.

However, times change, new voices are waiting to be heard and we social scientists must at least contextualize if not move with, the *Zeitgeist*.

It is important to resist the potential backlash towards essentialism and, as such, this book attempts to constitute a symbiosis with cultural studies and a constructive response to the appropriations of the postmodern. However, an acceptance of certain rapidly changing structural conditions does not necessarily lead to an abandonment of modernity's project any more than it demands a slavish obeisance to its ageing aspirations. A new politic needs to emerge and to speak with sufficient authority to quell the indistinguishable polysemy of the popular surface. Treated as a mere dwelling place for all and any manifestation of difference in social life, the idea of subculture becomes no more than an opinion – everyone has one and, as the cliché runs, they are entitled to it!

Enter Subculture

In this study, I will seek to establish that the cumulative contemporary fascination with culture itself has a social history. And, further, that the study of culture need not be exclusive, it does not demand the abandonment of the concepts of society and social structure. The debate will range from suggestions of integration to recommendations of contest, but it will essentially revolve around the necessity of interface. This discussion, I trust, will be timely as many humanities and social science degrees now incorporate the work of cultural studies and, indeed, cultural studies has quite successfully established itself as a part of many universities' academic profiles.

The mediating concept selected to organize these sets of concerns is that of *subculture*. In a substantive sense this work might serve a further purpose, namely to stand in an historical and perspectival relation to Dick Hebdige's milestone text *Subculture: The Meaning of Style*, first published in 1979. Hebdige's excellent work, though in many ways historically specific, has evolved, ironically, into an orthodoxy. His ethnographic case studies of punks, mods, teds and rastas are clearly reminiscent of an earlier era and his conceptualization of the central analytic issues in terms of Gramsci via Althusser (with interventions from Situationism) have also been outstripped by more contemporary developments in social, cultural and political theory. As tends to be the way with orthodoxies, they assume a canonical status, so much so that contemporary students sometimes assume that Hebdige discovered subcultures, both practically and in classificatory terms! My aim here is not to modernize Hebdige and produce an up-to-date inventory of subcultures containing youthful resistance. Rather, I would like to demonstrate the place of subculture as a concept in the development of social and cultural theory, to point to the reasoning behind its selection as an analytical and descriptive vehicle, in a variety of locations, and to reveal its ambivalent and perhaps unintentional contribution to the deconstruction of the concept 'society'. It is in this context that this work will confront its primary concern, that is, the politics of knowledge.

At its most straightforward we might suggest that following in the wake of Richard Hoggart's neo-Leavisite representation of working-class England's folkways and mores in *The Uses of Literacy* (1985), the scholars focused around the Birmingham Centre for Contemporary Cultural Studies (CCCS) group mobilized the idea of subculture to articulate the unspoken, or perhaps unheard, voices of a populist proletariat within a critical vision and still with an eye to radical social change. The arrival of Stuart Hall provided the drive and the impetus of that group and his particular version of Marxism provided the theoretical framework. The whole Birmingham CCCS tradition (now abruptly concluded, see Chapter 6), however, seemed largely content to restrict the idea of subculture to the pastime and possession of youth and, for some of its indigenous critics (McRobbie, 1981; Gilroy, 1987), mostly male youth:

> There have been studies of the relation of male youth to class and class culture, to the machinery of the State, and to the school, community and workplace. Football has been analyzed as a male sport, drinking as a male form of leisure, and the law and the police as patriarchal structures concerned with young male (potential) offenders. I don't know of a study that considers, never mind prioritises, youth and the family; women and the whole question of sexual division have been marginalised. (McRobbie, 1981: 111)

and perhaps even white male youth:

> Its voices present not so much a phantom history of post-war 'race relations' but a substantive history of its own – a history that shows the necessarily complex relationships which have existed between blacks and the cultural and political institutions of the white, urban working-class communities that are transformed and reoriented by their presence. (Gilroy, 1987: 154–5)

In such a context the previously powerful device presented in the form of the concept 'subculture' begins to degrade. As such, it becomes interpretable as little more than the noise of white, male adolescence, irksome at times but reparable through maturation. This hardly seems to provide a forceful platform for the reconstitution of a modern society nor an important ground, other than in partial and developmental terms, for the critical address of stratification. We will hear much more of this body of work in Chapter 6.

But the concept subculture did not begin either with Hebdige or the Birmingham group. Subculture is a concept with a long, but largely forgotten, history. What I would like to achieve in this work is an archaeology of the concept 'subculture' that will trace elements of the idea even to within the classic sociological tradition. That is, I will excavate the devices employed by the founding fathers to reconcile the desired stability of the post-Revolutionary European society with the inevitable recognition of accelerative and compound social change wrought through modernity's relentless progress. Thus, for example, Emile Durkheim's vision of the multiple mechanisms of workgroups and guilds functioning as a microcosm for the overall interdependence of organic solidarity. This discussion will take place in Chapter 2.

At a different stage in the development of our discipline, the Chicago School in the USA made strenuous efforts to elevate the life-world of the 'underdog' into an intelligible, yet manageable, form through urban studies, biographical methods, social reaction theory, labelling theory, typification vignettes and essentially through the assembling device of the subculture. At its most modest the Chicago School (or what we might describe more accurately as the neo-Chicago School following George Herbert Mead and Everett C. Hughes) can be seen to employ the concept of subculture to highlight the symbolic normative structure of groups smaller than the society as a whole. This is a micro-sociology, or perhaps a microcosmic sociology, that gives voice to and directs our attention to the ways in which such groups differ in such elements as their language, belief systems, values, mannerisms, patterns of behaviour and lifestyle from the mainstream, larger society, of which they are also a part. The formative insights of Chicago's long and influential tradition of sociology will be addressed in Chapter 3.

From a wholly different political position Talcott Parsons claimed the concept of subculture and incorporated it in a masterly fashion within the cybernetics and autopoeisis of *The Social System* so that all deviant and non-normatively oriented conduct could be absorbed within the scheme of central values. This was no simple diversion, it was this arresting appropriation of the concept of subculture that informed much of the positivist criminology and social pathology emanating from the USA and setting the ground rules for this sub-discipline up to the late 1950s. What we have here is a much more conflictual model.

The subculture is not a part within a part within a whole. In the Parsonian universe, central values stay central and the concept of a subculture designates a group, an enclave, a cult or a distraction of antithetical values that are expressions of either frustrations with or interventions into the dominant structure of legitimation and control within society. These are usually realized in terms of the pathological relationship between social structure and personality and are largely viewed in a remedial manner. The Parsonian, East Coast, approach to subculture will be explained in Chapter 4.

The very idea of a subculture re-emerged in the British sociology of education (Hargreaves, 1967; Lacey, 1970) in the late 1960s, as we shall see in Chapter 5. Here it was mobilized as a way of accounting for working-class under-achievement, this model being an unhappy amalgam of Chicago and Boston (in the form of Parsons) seen above.

Modern Origins of the Concept 'Subculture'

Definitions and versions proliferate and origins are obscure. It has been argued by Wolfgang and Ferracuti (1967) that the term 'subculture', though not the concept (a fine distinction), was not widely employed in the social science literature until after the Second World War. Lee (1945) is cited as making the first use of the term closely followed by Gordon (1947), who gives the definition of subculture as:

> a subdivision of a national culture, composed of a combination of factorable social situations such as class status, ethnic background, regional and rural or urban residence, and religious affiliation, but forming in their combination a functional unity which has an integrated impact on the participating individual. (Gordon, 1947: 40)

Another definition from around the same time states that:

> The term 'subculture' refers ... to 'cultural variants displayed by certain segments of the population'. Subcultures are distinguished not by one or two isolated traits – they constitute relatively cohesive social systems. They are worlds within the larger world of our national culture. (Komarovsky and Sargent, 1949: 143)

And so we evolve through: 'A society contains numerous subgroups, each with its own characteristic ways of thinking and acting. These cultures within cultures are called subcultures' (Mercer, 1958: 34) to 'Such shared learned behaviors which are common to a specific group or category are called subcultures' (Young and Mack, 1959: 49).

These examples are not isolated, the history of the concept comprises a vivid mosaic but each segment demonstrates a political move, and each exemplar reveals a step outside of the kernel sense of the social, for supportive or critical reasons, and the beginning of a gradient that leads through fragmentation towards agency. Of necessity, then, the concepts of identity, difference and selfhood will be addressed and from within a post-structuralist paradigm the politics of knowledge are now reviewed in terms of identity politics, affinity politics, standpoint epistemologies and the narratives of post-colonialism. Each of these moments is itself held in a tension with tenuous clusterings of the social, or rather the subcultural and we look to the heroic potentialities for liberation within the groupings of, for example, women, 'queer' folk, black consciousness, childhood or even cyborgs. The excavation of the tradition is not meant simply as an interesting but arcane history of an idea but rather as an argument for the necessity of a theory or mode of concept formation that enables what has come to be known as the middle range. That is, I will present a sociological argument for the place of an order of construct, like subculture, which retains the causal necessity of the social but overcomes the mysterious leap between, for example, Durkheim's structural constraints (the outside) and an individual act of self-destruction (the inside). Such argument both retains the necessity of the social and relocates the subcultural.

As long ago as 1960, in the USA, Yinger wrote:

In recent years there has been widespread and fruitful employment of the concept of subculture in sociological and anthropological research. The term has been used to focus attention not only on the wide diversity of norms to be found in many societies but on the normative aspects of deviant behavior. The ease with which the term has been adopted, with little study of its exact meanings or its values and its difficulties, is indicative of its utility in emphasizing a sociological point of view in research that has been strongly influenced both by individualistic and moralistic interpretations. To describe the normative qualities of an occupation, to contrast the value systems of social classes, or to emphasize the controlling power of the code of a delinquent gang is to underline a sociological aspect of those phenomena that is often disregarded. (1960: 625)

These remarks are in large part supportive of the endeavour of a number of subcultural theorists to honour the norms, life ways and values of members of some groups which at a systems level might be disregarded as dysfunctional, irrational, sick or deviant. However, addressing more meta-theoretical considerations he continues:

> It is unfortunate that 'subculture,' a central concept in this process, has seldom been adequately defined. It has been used as an *ad hoc* concept whenever a writer wished to emphasize the normative aspects of behavior that differed from some general standard. The result has been a blurring of the meaning of the term, confusion with other terms, and a failure frequently to distinguish between two levels of social causation. (Yinger, 1960: 625–6)

I would agree with this point. We cannot simply elect to define a group of people whose proximity or range of activities has fallen under our analytic gaze as a subculture unless we express a clear epistemological purpose. Now if that purpose is to indicate the very difference of that group of people or the conscious antagonism of that group of people to what the body of people in their wider society think or believe, then, as Yinger (1960) points out, we might properly employ the concept of a 'contraculture'. Perhaps the purpose of subcultural work is to demonstrate inconsistencies between a particular group's practices and that of the mainstream and to reveal further the systematic strategies that they employ to guarantee a reproduction of those inconsistencies, then we may be implying that subcultures exercise agency, their difference is self-consciously meaningful action, in which case might not they be potentially 'asocial'? However far we push the definitional necessity of subcultures bearing a relationship to some sense of a wider normative structure (be that a soft or hard conceptualization), then we are still left with the problem of boundaries. Downes, interrogating the concept in relation to an explanation of delinquent activity, expresses this well:

> [N]o culture can be regarded as a completely integrated system. Most cultures, like personalities, can be regarded as permeated by apparent contradictions.
>
> The concept of the 'subculture' embodies one such contradiction. What constitutes the 'culture' of a complex society: all its subcultures, their uniformities only, or the dominant subculture? Where, to put it crudely, does culture end and subculture begin? Does subculture merely refract or totally displace culture? Any vagueness over the boundaries of the overall culture will automatically extend to subcultures. (1966: 4–5)

Downes continues to address the elusive nature of this boundary yet is drawn to proceed in his criminological analysis on the basis of his own typology which, though clear, continues to avoid the question that he himself has raised. He says that subcultures may be classified into two main kinds, one of which contains two sub-categories:

> (a) those which precede, or are formed *outside* the context of the 'dominant culture': for example, the 'culture' of immigrant groups which become 'subcultures' in the context of the host culture; also, regional subcultures which precede, but come to co-exist, merge with or differentially respond to the enveloping 'dominant culture'.
> (b) those which originate *within* the context of the dominant culture: these fall into two sub-categories:
> (i) those which emerge in *positive* response to the demands of the social and cultural structures; for example, occupational subcultures, age-group subcultures, and
> (ii) those emerging in *negative* response to the social and cultural structures' demands; e.g. delinquent subcultures; religious-messianic-revivalist subcultures; political-extremist subcultures. (ibid.: 9)

One of the evasions here is concerning the internal coherence and ontological status of such subcultures, that is, are we to assume that the members of such groups know that they are members of such groups and that such groups actually exist as reality structures? The other evasion concerns the epistemological status of such subcultures, that is, are they all, in a significant sense, actually theoretical devices used to formulate collective action for specific rhetorical, political or moral purposes?

Subculture: The Analytic Problem

Although the motivation to describe and explain slices of life in the mould of subcultures may, in most non-Parsonian instances, be to insulate, to ideal-type, to retain a difference and an essence, to politicize and to render equivalent, it is also a dereliction of the sociologist's commitment to explain the social in terms of the social (or at least engage with the problems that such an imperative entails). In one strong sense the invocation of the concept of subculture to explain a social phenomenon is an analytic sidestep or swerve by the theorist to avoid the crunching impact with the social structure and its claim for mono-causality. Now the situation is clearly not an either/or but without the buttress of intervening theorizing about levels, constraint and social control, and to opt non-reflexively for the use of subculture as a source of explanation begins a reduction. The path to individualistic reductionism started here leads to the ultimate abandonment of a sociological per-spective by arguing that an event occurred 'because this subculture is unique', 'because that's the kind of guy he is' or 'because one or more individuals are mad'.

Perhaps the story begins rather further back. Totalizing concepts like 'society' and 'social systems' have never had a practical currency within the explanatory frameworks of lay members of any particular social group. Perhaps we might argue that since the 1960s, in the West, 'society' has become part of a quasi-political rhetoric of mitigation for the unwanted or unintended consequences of human action. It desig-nates a dull, deep-seated, impersonal causality for which no one person has to claim unique responsibility. Even at times of severe external threat, like war, when Durkheim convincingly predicted that social soli-darity would reach an unprecedented intensity, it is empirically unlikely that previously experienced forms of difference, stratification, inclu-sion and exclusion would become resolved through more than the expressive mode of a new and transitory sense of nationhood. Society, then, is essentially an analytical device both contrived and espoused by sociology in its earliest incarnations, to establish the specific and distinct ontology that all scientific paradigms require to announce their difference from all previous types of understanding. Society is a struc-turalist trope routinely employed to designate and summarize all of the universal, ideal, essential and peculiarly human dispositions that ensure their tendency to opt for clustering rather than isolation. More than this, society is an inevitable growth out of moral philosophy that saves humankind from the sad and shallow reductions that are required through its explanation with reference to psychology's 'behaviour', 'market forces' in economics, and 'the state' in politics. The actual empirical referent of 'society' is people's perpetual, though variable, sense of the 'social' and 'sociality'. The praise and illumination of this fine and irrepressible human sentiment were sociology's rightful purpose at its inception, not some cynical attempt at intellectual entrepreneurship or epistemological imperialism. And this is worthy of retention.

Real, material people know about love, attraction, affection, care, altruism, obligation, contracting, expectation, togetherness, solidarity, loyalty, belonging, and so on, without being able to, or indeed needing to, point at an object form called society. Sociologists speak of society while lay members know about and act in relation to family, friendship, community, organization, institution and group membership. Clearly, what is at work here is not a confusion or a competition between dif-ferent reality structures, nor even the existence of a parallel world. In reality, what we are witnessing is the practice of construction or transformation from one order, the 'lived', into another order, the 'conceptual'. This transformation implies no hierarchy of validity, but certainly the latter seeks to understand more fully the former and to do so by extraction, clarification, and releasing the everyday world from the grip of the common sense (or what ethnomethodology would refer to as the taken-for-granted). In a strong sense, then, the sociologist's invocation of 'society' makes reference to the lay member's cognitive and affective architecture which enables his or her bonding with others.

It has been argued that the signifier 'society' implies a description of a nation–state or a population, but this is relatively worthless in attempting to discern meaning. Nation–states are historical, arbitrary, sometimes geographical and almost always internally divisive units symbolically united by language – sometimes. Population, on the other hand, is a strictly statistical category. Demographic trends are *post hoc* descriptions of stability or instability, they are not explanations of meaningful human action and motive.

Society must remain an ideal conceptualization of a collective consciousness which exerts constraint upon individual action with the function of sustaining groups, formations and networks of interaction. This is the level that sociologists have continued to refer to as the 'macro' as opposed to the 'micro'. Any shift towards the micro, as is instanced by the espousal of the term 'subculture' must take care not to liberate its object of study from the constraints of the totality. Subcultures cannot in any sense be meaningfully insulated from the society of which they are an inevitable part. Subcultural theories are obliged to express their coherence with social theories from which they have emerged.

Thornton addressing a similar range of concerns states the following:

> What is a 'subculture'? What distinguishes it from a 'community'? And what differentiates these two social formations from the 'masses', the 'public', 'society', 'culture'? These are obstinate questions to which there is no agreed answer, but rather a debate – the problem at the root of which is about how scholars imagine and make sense of people, not as individuals, but as members of discrete populations or social groups. Studies of subcultures are attempts to map the social world and, as such, they are exercises in representation. In attempting to depict the social world or translate it into sociology (or cultural studies or any of the other disciplines that are active in the field), we are unavoidably involved in a process of construction. (Gelder and Thornton: 1997: 1)

But she goes on to say: '"Community" is perhaps the label whose referent is closest to subculture, to the degree that several contributors use the term interchangeably. Nevertheless, there are subtle disparities between the two concepts, which affect when and why one or the other is applied in any case' (ibid.: 2). She then reminds us that communities conventionally suggest a greater permanence than subcultures, that they tend to be geographically aligned to a specific locale, and that in general they comprise of families and kinship groups. All of this is coherent with what we came to know as British community studies through, for example, the work of Young and Wilmott (1957), Wilmott (1966), Townsend (1957) and Jackson and Marsden (1962). However, there is a more analytic point to be made which is illuminated by Harris when he says:

> Community is an old and venerable sociological concept that developed in sociology's 'classic period' and has only recently begun to be problematised. It is, moreover, one area of debate within which sociology can plausibly claim to be part of the 'reflexivity of modernity'. Community is a concept with powerful resonances among non-sociologists, and lay and sociological uses inform each other. To call something a community is to link it into an intense signifying chain with positive connotations such as locality, solidarity, closeness and mutual support. (2001: 37)

Group Classifications

What this opens up is a further, an important, distinction in the classifications that sociologists might employ which is often confused or conflated in the application of the concept subculture. We can attempt to classify different forms of social group and we can attempt to classify different forms of social relationship. The former is about scale and proximity, the latter is about texture and integration.

When we speak about classifying social groups, we might make reference to Simmel's (1902) highly sophisticated micro-sociology, his analyses of the dynamics within dyads and triads and his exposition of the interwoven links between the physical size of a group, the organization or structure of a group and character of the relationships that exist within such groups. All this Simmel refers to as 'the quantitative determination of certain divisions and of certain groups'. Much later, Homans (1948) attempted a not wholly satisfactory taxonomy of human groups based not so much on how they diverge as on the ways in which they overlap. This was a micro-sociological attempt to elicit high-level generalizations concerning the nature of social interaction. Subsequently, Gurvich set out an extremely abstract and complex matrix through which different types of social group may be determined:

> It is clear that every organised group is also structured. However, a group may not only be structurable, but also structured, without also being organised, nor even capable of being organised, not even capable of being expressed in a single organisation (such as social classes, which are a patent example of this). Further, when organisation enters into the equilibrium of a structure, it is no more than one element, and not even an indispensable one at that. (Gurvich, 1957: 60)

He discusses fifteen criteria which include size, proximity, duration, function, and so on. The scheme claims to be exhaustive.

When we speak about classifying different forms of social relationship, we enter into a far less cold, technical and empirical realm (though this would not be a fair way to describe Simmel's work which is equally instructive about the texture of relationships). In this context we are aggregating and disaggregating different manners of relationship, social bond or solidarity. It is in this context that classical sociological theory has made some of its most telling and lasting pronouncements. We shall be addressing this contribution to our overall thesis in detail in Chapter 2 but it is necessary to provide a brief inventory here to sediment the overall idea. Perhaps most noticeably Durkheim, in his thesis on the division of labour in society (1964a), provided us with two formative modes of collection and integration that he referred to as 'mechanical' and 'organic' solidarity. These were intangible entities yet experienced as the social sentiments of societal members; sociologically, these are powerful devices for establishing a link between the social bond and the symbolic order in terms of both chronology and complexity. Mechanical solidarity is a highly condensed symbolic experience and organic is much more diffuse, one may well evolve from the former, both absolutely fit the going order and both appropriately demonstrate the intense interrelation between action, affect and social structure. Even before Durkheim, Tönnies (1887) had developed his thesis which distinguished between *Gemeinschaft* and *Gesellschaft*, concepts which have come to be transposed as ideal-typical representations of 'community' and 'association' (or 'society'). This two-fold scheme can and has been applied to the distinction between groups as well as the distinction between societies but, as in the case of Durkheim, the idea was clearly inspired by the advent and march of modernity along an evolutionary yet unpredictable path. And earlier still, in 1876, the anthropologist Sir Henry Maine drew an enlightening separation between those societies whose relationships are ordered by 'status' and those that are ordered by 'contract'. In Maine's writing this primary distinction parallels a second, namely, the distinction between 'static' and 'progressive' societies. The gradient from stasis to progress is often specified by the development of civil laws which shift the focus of control from the individual to the family. There are striking homologies between these various lines of theorizing, as we shall soon see.

The idea of subculture will, then, take us to a range of places and open up a spectrum of debate. What I shall not attempt is an exhaustive account of the concept in all its manifestations, that could become tedious and not particularly informative. Nearly a quarter of a century ago Mike Brake produced a fine inventory of the applications of the concept in relation to youth and popular culture which left him confident enough to direct us forward with this 'new' taxonomy:

> Subcultural theory has developed considerably since the mid-sixties. It can be divided into four approaches. First, there is the early social ecology of the working-class neighbourhood carried out in the late fifties and early sixties. Second, there is the relation of the delinquent subculture to the sociology of education, a tradition which is still continuing. This examines the relationship of leisure and youth culture as an alternative to achievement in the school. Third, there is the cultural emphasis of the Centre for Contemporary Cultural Studies at Birmingham University. This approach, which is influenced by the new criminology developed by the National Deviancy Conferences, used a Marxist framework to consider youth cultures and their style, in terms of their relationship to class, dominant culture and ideology. Involved in this is the attempt to examine the ethnography of youth culture, their relation to popular culture and their moments in class history. Lastly there are the contemporary neighbourhood studies which look at local youth groups, not as the early social ecologists did, but in the light of influence by contemporary deviancy theory and social reaction. Both of these approaches consider the meaning that youth cultures and subcultures have for their members. (Brake, 1980: 50)

We will be looking at this set of developments, some in much more detail than others, but with the aim of eliciting certain pervasive theoretical themes. It is this level of the overall contribution to sociological theory that will be our prime objective, not a detailed exposition of particular empirical studies, though some of these will be included precisely because they are illustrative of the more abstract issues.

It is in the light of this primary analytical objective that the book will conclude with a discussion of the subcultural concept's contribution to the instability of sociological explanations and a perceived diminution of faith in the causal significance of 'society' in our modern accounts. Inevitably, then, our conclusions will draw us into a discussion of postmodernism and its implications for sociological reason.

As we have come to see, any discussion of postmodernism has to begin with a discussion of what modernity is and has been. The concept of subculture will be employed in the context of this debate to see these wider issues in relation to ourselves as temporal, that is as operating through a time consciousness, but also to our positioning in space. Modernity may well be an incomplete project but we are therefore left with a series of contemporary politics that fall into all the traps that postmodernity sets up for them. Not least that pitfall concerning morality which is difficult to reconstitute on a subcultural basis. Where to take politics now? How to make judgements concerning the 'good' on grounds which are other than short-term or merely pragmatic?

TWO Trace Elements in the Classic Tradition

When we investigate the times and social currents in which sociology has emerged, we encounter a paradoxical relationship with the modern. The project of modernity, albeit without a written constitution, was nevertheless describing itself across Europe in the forms of capitalism, industrialization, bureaucratization, urbanization and ever refined modes of the division of labour. Sociology, the critical philosophy of its age, was engaged with the post-Enlightenment metaphysic of progress, much accelerated by Hegel, yet equally on the side of humanist ethics of freedom, equality and a strong sense of the celebration of human togetherness. In one sense, then, it provided a description and analysis of modernity's tactics but it also proffered a critique of the damage that modernity's advance threatened if left unrestrained. 'Moral reality, like all reality, can be studied from two different points of view. One can set out to explore and understand it and one can set out to evaluate it. The first of these problems, which is theoretical, must necessarily precede the second' (Durkheim, 1974: 35).

It would appear then that sociology is inevitably caught by its antithesis. Its authority arises from an appraisal of what it seeks to critique. It speaks through categories that are already of its time and therefore, in a sense, part of the problem rather than part of the solution. This is not a problem unique to sociology, nearly two centuries ago, Hegel had noted its ironic inevitability as a feature of all philosophical endeavour:

> Philosophy always comes on the scene too late to give instructions as to what the world ought to be. As the thought of the world, it appears only when actuality is already there, cut and dried, after its process of formation has been completed ... When philosophy paints its grey on grey, then a shape of life has grown old. It cannot be rejuvenated by philosophy' grey

on grey; it can only be understood. It is only with the fall of dusk that the owl of Minerva spreads its wings. (Hegel, *The Philosophy of Right*, 1820)

This was perhaps not challenged until Nietzsche and the post-structuralisms that came in his wake. What this all means in practical terms is that although modern sociology espouses, nay eulogizes, reflexivity and critical self-investigation, it is often, nevertheless, forgetful of the grounds of its own narrative voice. How else could a discipline so committed to challenging the going order for so long succumb to the dominant ideologies so that stratifications marked out by gender and ethnicity remained part of its central vocabulary? As late as the 1960s and the 1970s, sociology in Europe began to question the adequacy of socio-economic based categories inherited from what we now call the modernist classical tradition, as being appropriate analytical vehicles to appraise social formations which were already metamorphosing into the postmodern.

Perhaps we just ask too much of our modern sociologies, perhaps there is an inevitable entropic decay built into sociology's project:

> Modernity's strength lay in having situated everything in the framework of History and historical development. 'Centrifugation' is nothing more than the intellectual translation of such a perspective. But what was once a strength has inevitably become a weakness. Indeed, History deprived histories their place; it relativized experience. And these once-repressed experiences are resurfacing today with a vengeance. Their modulations are of all types, but with a common thread favouring empiricism and proxemics. This is forcing us to reorient our analyses, to focus our scrutiny on 'the most extreme concrete' (W. Benjamin) that is everyday life. (Maffesoli, 1996: 163)

If this is indeed the case, then a concept such as 'subculture' is just one more staging place on the way through fragmentation to dispersion and asociality. But perhaps not; let us take a hard look at the gathering social metaphors of classical sociology and use them to reflect upon more recent theorist's choice to employ the concept of a subculture.

Tönnies's Binary: *Gemeinschaft* and *Gesellschaft*

Tönnies, as far back as 1887, made a now canonical distinction between two manifestations of the social bond. These two types of union between people he referred to as 'community' (*Gemeinschaft*) and 'society' or 'association' (*Gesellschaft*). These classificatory forms have, through the years, been employed in a number of ways which we might summarize as follows:

1 The distinction between types of human relation e.g. 'intimate' and 'dispersed'.
2 The distinction between types of agglomeration or proximity e.g. 'rural' and 'urban'.
3 The distinction between actual types of society, e.g. 'traditional' and 'modern'.

And in many useful ways, Tönnies's analytical model serves all of these purposes well. The concepts are essentially heuristic devices rather than empirical descriptions and, as such, retain a fluidity and a nimbleness that allows for such adaptation and relocation. As Tönnies himself puts it: 'both names are in the present context stripped of their connotation as designating social entities or groups, or even collective or artificial people; the essence of both Gemeinschaft and Gesellschaft is found interwoven in all kinds of associations' (Tönnies, 1955: 18 quoted in Harris, 2001: 37).

Within the idea of *Gemeinschaft* we can assemble such affective traits as privacy, inclusion, exclusivity and, as previously cited, intimacy. Extending from this focus we can align more concrete forms such as families, clans, kinship groups and perhaps build into neighbourhoods and friendship groups and networks. *Gesellschaft*, however, in signifying association, calls on notions of public as opposed to private life. Such relationality depends upon the exercise of cognition rather than the feelings, it is about consciousness, deliberation and rational choice. There is a gradient of intentionality gradually disclosed behind these two forms of bonding, they conjure up two different forms of human will or motivation (perhaps prefiguring Max Weber's 'traditional' and 'instrumental' rationalities). Timasheff puts it thus:

> All social relations are creations of human will, of which there are two types. The first is the essential will: the basic, instinctive, organic tendency which drives human activity as from behind. The second is arbitrary will: the deliberate, purposive form of volition which determines human activity with regard to the future. Essential will, Toennies stresses, dominates the life of peasants and artisans or 'common' people, while arbitrary will characterizes the activities of business men, scientists, persons of authority and members of the upper class. (1955: 100)

What is critical here in relation to our modernist sociology thesis is that the dimension extending between *Gemeinschaft* and *Gesellschaft* is transversed by economic interest. That is, 'communities' are made up of individuals whose total identity is proscribed by the sentiment of the collectivity whereas the 'association' is opted into with a motivation towards partial and wholly specific outcomes and it is united through a reciprocal and rational agreement of interest – the latter has much more the characteristics of the market or the division of labour.

This economic dimension is important when assessing the modernist elements of growth and change embodied in the concepts. *Gesellschaft* results, in part, from a development into complexity. This is a stage when the needs of *Gemeinschaft* are no longer satisfied and the burgeoning wants of *Gesellschaft* become available through exchange in a wider context. Both as part of but also because of the advancing division of labour individuals and the goods or services that they offer become voluntarily detached from the stasis of community. The new meeting point becomes the free market and economic exchange, symbolic exchange and social exchange blur into a new form of commonality and association. And so the form of the bond appears driven by the socio-economic vectors, material circumstances come to proscribe the parameters around the way that people relate. European capitalism truly makes the society and we get the society that our capitalist will deserves. Although there appears to be longings in Tönnies's work (as in Durkheim's to follow) for the mode of relationality, *Gemeinschaft*, now outstripped, there is an implicit recognition of the difficulty in reversing this historical current. Various cheap, ideological attempts at such social engineering have been attempted such as Hitler's claim for the *Heimweh* to emerge through National Socialism and Margaret Thatcher's appeal for a return to Victorian values; being both purely rhetorical and hopelessly romantic, they have failed.

In a sense, then, what begins as a dichotomous classification, a structuralist move often replicated in subsequent social theories, reforms into a continuum and one that is tolerant of overlap. Thus, we can see that it may be virtually impossible to achieve the pure status of a *Gemeinschaft* community yet within a *Gesellschaft* society there are a number of *Gemeinschaft* points at which the individual engages the social and announces his or her unique personal, yet wholly social, identity. Similarly, in a nation or state, almost demographic in character, certain mechanisms can induce the *Gemeinschaft* sentiment of, say, national consciousness. What this enables conceptually, however, is a community or communities coexistent within a society. This model sustains and announces its difference to the concept of subculture because of the emphasis on the will but also because of the sustained theorizing concerning the symbolic order of the social structure. That is, *Gemeinschaft* sentiments arise in a reciprocal relation to *Gesellschaft* sensations of bonding.

> Since *Gemeinschaft* and *Gesellschaft* correspond to types of will, social relations are treated by Toennies as manifestations of these. Human wills may enter into manifold relations, with the emphasis on either preservation of order or on its destruction; but only the former, relations of reciprocal affirmation, should be studied by sociologists. Reciprocal affirmation itself varies in intensity. Thus a social state exists if two persons will to be in a definite relationship; this relationship is commonly recognized also by others. When a social state obtains between more than two persons, there is a circle. If, however, individuals are regarded as forming a unit because of common natural or psychic traits, they form a collective. Finally, if there is organization assigning specific functions to definite persons, the social body becomes a corporation. According to Toennies, all of these social formations may be based either on essential will or on arbitrary will. It is, however, hard to conceive how a collective could be a *Gesellschaft* or a corporation a *Gemeinschaft*. (Timasheff, 1955: 100–1)

Tönnies, then appears, quite early on in our tradition, to have opened up the possibility of sociology attending to different levels at which humankind can experience the social. Even though his two major concepts, which are still employed today, do not exhaust the extraordinary variations that characterize people's collective life, it provides a model with fluidity which nevertheless honours a strong sense of social structure. The many parts are not hermetically sealed. This has been an instructive landmark on the way to subcultures and alerts us to the significance of both openness and closure, and the fluidity enabling any movement between these two possibilities in our conceptualizations of the social bond. Urry (2000) develops a sociology of mobilities which both investigates this fluidity but insists that the previously assumed stasis of fixed social institutions is no longer applicable to a global society. The very idea of mobility redescribes social life in irregular and unstable ways:

> community is also a matter of powerful discourses and metaphors. Certain ideals of a supposed *Gemeinschaft* are vigorously attached to particular social groupings, especially in recent years in western societies with the supposed general loss of community and its communion-like features. But many places that deploy the notion of community are often of course characterised by highly unequal internal social relations and by

exceptional hostility to those who are on the outside. To speak of community is to speak metaphorically or ideologically. (Urry, 2000: 134)

Despite this most recent reconfiguration we will find that Tönnies's
dichotomous taxonomy set a pattern often replicated in social thought
though sometimes moulded into a triadic classification, so, for example, Sir Henry Maine's 'status' and 'contract'; Herbert Spencer's 'militant' and 'industrial'; Charles Cooley's 'primary groups' and 'others',
Karl Popper's 'tribal' and 'open'; Hobhouse's 'kinship', 'authority' and
'citizenship'; Max Weber's 'traditional', 'charismatic' and 'bureau-
cratic'; Herman Schmalenbach's 'community', 'federation' and 'society';
and Georges Gurvitch's 'communion', 'community' and 'mass', to name
but a few. We shall revisit some of these later but our next stop will be
with perhaps the most famous of them all within classical sociology.

Durkheim: Society as a Form of Solidarity

Emile Durkheim (1858–1917) set our analytical problem for us in a
whole series of ways. It was Durkheim, largely through his early work,
writing what has been termed a sociological realism, who gave us our
sustaining legacy of 'society' itself. It was this iconic gift, or for many
this suffocating burden, that launched the discipline that we variously
inhabit. His whole edifice was in fact not simple realism but rather a
complex analytic scheme of tangible possibilities nevertheless
inspired by Comte's positivism and the desire for an empirical proof
fit to qualify a new science.

At around the turn of the nineteenth century Durkheim opened up
a new territory for our attention and conscious occupation – this was
'society' *sui generis*. Philosophical, political and economic paradigms
extending back to the pre-Socratics had addressed the ordered relations
between people but Durkheim originally maps, through his science of
ethics, the social 'world'. This is an ontological space, a source of
causality, and the primary context for the functioning of all previously
considered theories of human conduct. It is this sacred ground that is
so easily surrendered or sold off in job lots for redevelopment as 'subcultures'. What Durkheim achieved at a more analytical level than
merely founding a discipline (though this is achievement enough) was
an awakening of a new moral, political and cognitive commitment to a
new conceptual place for humankind, albeit modern humankind, to
inhabit. Many previous nineteenth-century explorers revealed whimsical

sights fit for the new tourist, be it traveller or taxonomer, but Durkheim's 'social' was hard, factual, contested and burgeoning with the propensities to both change and explode. This was no space for the tourist, but rather a battleground for the social scientist *qua* moral scientist. So compelling were the images in interlocking constellations he laid before us that their existence, though not their interpretation, has gone without challenge until the end of the twentieth century. This latter-day assault on the social world has emerged as part of a Western manifestation of egoism in the form of retro-eighteenth-century economic theory, and also as a dimension of de-traditionalization in Baudrillard's conception of the post-. Both of these challenges were, incidentally, anticipated in Durkheim's corpus of work through his concepts of 'forced' and 'anomic' divisions of labour:

> the potential to reopen modernist closure is not found in the lax pluralities of many 'posterities' but in the rather more awkward constraints of Durkheim's notions of solidarity and the normative. The impulses of much postmodern theory are too ironic, too ready, like Baudrillard to keep 'simulacra' within the index of negativity and alienation, too ready like Lyotard to define the sublime in terms of an act of continued negation. (Smith, in Jenks, 1995: 253)

Durkheim's vision was both complex and truly 'visionary'. His irony is, however, that his thought has become ideologically *passé*. Crude appropriations of Durkheim manage his ideas as simply positivist, functionalist and essentially conservative. Undergraduates rail at his holism, his totalizing effects and his disregard for the individual identity and personality. Rather more sophisticated, yet still conventional, views of Durkheim treat his work diachronically and at three different levels. First, *substantively* his concerns are understood as demonstrating a shift from institutions to beliefs. Second, his work is gathered *theoretically* within an evolutionary thesis, that is, his manifest preoccupation with the transition from simple societies into the form of complex societies. It is suggested through constructing a rigid framework of morphologies that he attempted to establish the functional conditions for the moral bond along an historical continuum. Finally, his *methodological* commitment is witnessed as a development from an early positivism, and indeed empiricism, through a series of analytic encounters which lead ultimately to the inappropriate character of this method and the emergence of a new, yet not entirely articulated, style of address. This chronology is well expressed by Parsons (1968) as Durkheim's movement from 'positivism' to 'idealism' – so we are presented with a version of an 'epistemological break'.

My argument here is twofold: first, it attempts to restore the remarkable and visionary character of the Durkheimian view. I will assert that all of Durkheim's work is coherent and principled. It does not simply demonstrate a change in substantive interests, it is not simply developmental in its theorizing of societal forms and it does not reveal an overthrow or defeat of an increasingly inappropriate sociological method. At a deep structural level Durkheim's whole project is unified and essential in its variety – its differences are homologous. And, second, I seek to emphasize the non-negotiable character of the concept of society and its manifestations in the experience of social structure that Durkheim has provided us with. Both of these strands of the argument are to be seen in relation to the development of the concept of subculture. It will be shown that Durkheim also recognized the need to theorize human conduct at a level below the demographically macro but that he maintained the necessity of accounting for such conduct in relation to structural constraints in excess of the experiential micro. He had no need for intermediary concepts like subculture, though it could be argued that he experienced certain problems in locating the origins of crime.

I would suggest that Durkheim's methodological programme may be viewed as occasioned by real social change – the experience of modernity and the threatening spectre of postmodernity – and perhaps, at one level, as attending concretely to that experience of change:

> Over and over again, Durkheim comments on the uneasiness, anxiety, malaise, disenchantment, pessimism, and other negative characteristics of his age. His comments on the leading proponents of the *fin de siècle* spirit – among them, Bergson, James, Nietzsche, and Guyau – are mixed with sympathy as well as outrage. But his remarks on the Enlightenment philosophers, Hobbes, Montesquieu, Rousseau, Comte, Kant, Saint-Simon, and others, are unequivocally critical with regard to their naivetè, optimism, and simplicity. (Mestrovic, 1991: 75)

However, at an analytic level, Durkheim's corpus generates different and predicted methods for different sets of problems which are, in turn, echoes of the two different manners through which people might realize their world. In this way Durkheim's insights are not linked specifically to the moment of their occurrence but have applicability to the rapidly transforming conditions of modernity into late modernity.

The methodological programme is provided with its models through Durkheim's thesis in *The Division of Labour* (1964a). This work will be regarded as grounding all of Durkheim's theorizing. I will argue that the two forms of solidarity revealed in Durkheim's text, the mechanical and the organic, may be treated as metaphors for different ways of being in the world, different ways of seeing and understanding the world, and thus for different sociological approaches to the world. Indeed, they are paradigmatic. It is not an original thought to link these two models with the binary we considered earlier in the form of Tönnies's *Gemeinschaft* and *Gesellschaft*. Both dyads are, at one level, descriptive of different modes of association and, at another level, evolutionary. Even though they can be taken as representative of different scales of social association there is no sense in which they are deemed to be either exclusive or antagonistic in the way that I am suggesting, more generally, that the concept of a subculture is.

These two possibilities arising from Durkheim I shall refer to as the 'mechanical' and 'organic' epistemologies of the two sociologies. The former, the mechanical, is a mode of both cognition and accounting that is preoccupied with description. This betrays an habitual realism with no distinction at work between objects-in-reality and objects-in-thought. It renders all understanding obedient to the criteria of literalism. This way of being is clearly primary to and celebrated through the twin traditions of positivism and empiricism that have engaged and stalked sociological reasoning, and subsequently mediated its relation to the wider culture, from its inception at the close of the nineteenth century up until its threatened fragmentation in the present day. Also instilled within the lexicon of the sociological analyst is the central metaphor of 'observation', deriving from the relations of mechanicism. Beyond these metatheoretical considerations, the mechanical epistemology bestows a particular, practical status upon the theorist, a status that enables such continuous literal description by and through the privileged difference of the sociologist. The sociologist is thus realized through expertise, the sociologist is as a high priest. This is the stance that Maffesoli (1996) criticizes as the 'scholasticism' of sociology and that others, including modern neo-Marxist subculture theorists, have regaled for imposing meaningless or lifeless groupings on everyday life. However, the sociologist needs to be reflexive about the locus of his or her responsibilities. The high priest's magic is not diminished by having a vocabulary not shared by the laity. I am pleased that my doctor knows more and differently from myself.

In the latter mode, the second yet simultaneous vision, that of the organic epistemology, we are offered understanding not through description but through espousal. Within organicism difference becomes accepted, it becomes conventional. The taken-for-grantedness of difference emerges as the grounds on which we begin to understand the other, thus difference itself must be regarded as a form of equivalence. In this context, the understanding of difference requires not the privileged description of that which is sundered from self, but an espousal in the dual sense of an analytic wedding to or sameness with the other and an adoption or indeed advocacy of that other's position. This approaches a sense of the exercise of elective instrumental will and a recognition of that motivation in others. The theorist now experiences a dramatic change in status; the reification of expert and high priest as describer of the mundane becomes itself secularized and a part of that realm of the mundane. The theorist becomes like Garfinkel, an espouser of and equivalent to the lay member. Similarly, the lay member is enjoined in the ethno-methodology of the sociologist to both artfully see, on a shared plane, and apprehend. Garfinkel's ethnomethodology is precisely a late-modern articulation of the intricacies of organicism. What modern sociology has called 'everyday life' is not a new realm; it is that predicted by the complexity of organicism and its emphasis on difference. Garfinkel acknowledges this continuity with Durkheim and shifts the focus of sociology from a description and analysis of external social structures to a description and analysis of the internal experience of social structures (or being structured). What both theorists retain is the centrality of 'society' as a motivating force unconstrained by the size or composition of the group which the actor is occupying. Subcultural theory, in common with Goffman's analysis of face-to-face encounters, forgets that this is not all a person does or knows in a day or indeed a lifetime.

Let us now return to Durkheim and work with the view that the two forms of solidarity, rather than being merely transitory descriptions of historical conditions, are metaphors for different forms of life, that is, different ontological orders, each giving rise to attendant and complementary epistemological rules of apprehension. Clearly, the forms of solidarity, treated as analytics, signified particular empirical referents, such as clans or states or whatever, and thus enabled Durkheim to account for real social change along an historical continuum; the inspiration for this change being the degree of moral density, and the key to decoding its form being the manner of aggregation. However, the point of my current reading is to elucidate the constitution of the two phenomenal models of social life which lead to two positions on method, two perspectives:

> Durkheim ... while remaining a defender of the primacy of the role of rea-
> son and the individual in society, he cannot help but note, de facto, the
> importance of sentiment and community. I believe that the distinction
> Durkheim makes between 'mechanical solidarity' and 'organic solidarity',
> and especially his application of these concepts, is no longer highly per-
> tinent. Rather, it is important to underline that he was truly obsessed by the
> reality represented by solidarity. This is no trifling matter ... it is certain that
> the problem of the pre-rational and pre-individualist consensus is for him
> a basis on which society can and will be built. From this stems the impor-
> tance he lends to the *conscience collective* or to specific moments (festi-
> vals, common acts) by which a given society will reinforce 'the feeling it
> has of itself'. (Maffesoli, 1996: 79)

I assemble here, for the sake of brevity, a set of binary oppositions instanced as the forms of solidarity but in turn instancing two different ways of seeing and ways of being in the world – what Wittgenstein might refer to as two 'forms of life'. These binary oppositions are, per-haps, best reviewed in Table 2.1.

We can now consider the transformation of these two models or forms of life, into methodological paradigms and subsequently high-light the distinct features of these two paradigms at work in the 'early' and 'late' phases of Durkheim's work. Both paradigms contain onto-logical and epistemological commitments; that is, assumptions con-cerning the nature of the phenomena of interest and also assumptions concerning the best ways of relating to such phenomena. This res-onates with Kuhn's (1970) notion of 'paradigmatic knowledge' in that they map out the parameters of knowing by providing rules for what is there to be observed and understood and what is not.

Within mechanical solidarity, our first model, we have a primary ontological commitment to the inherent order in the social world. This order is an essential metaphysic which is mobilized, in human terms, through the pre-social yet gregarious urges of the 'primitive horde'. Humankind is disposed to sociality by virtue of it's species being, and a person's experience of him/herself and of others within that sociality is through and by virtue of the social bond. The social bond, which is based on resemblance (a pragmatic ordering principle), is maintained by a strong collective consciousness. The collective consciousness is, in turn, transcendent – it is projected out as God (an unquestioning order-ing principle). The *a priori* status of the deity is not contentious in mechanical solidarity, people and their understandings are held in check by faith – the world is experienced as inherently ordered; humankind itself is contingent upon that order. Such conservation of

Table 2.1 Mechanical and organic solidarity

Mechanical solidarity	Organic solidarity
predominant in more simple societies	predominant in more advanced societies
characterized by homogeneity, likeness	characterized by heterogeneity, difference
social bond based on resemblance	social bond based on interdependence
segmented structure – clans, tribes	organized aggregate structure – cities and states
belief system religious, transcendental Gods	scientific knowledge, secular ideologies
strong collective consciousness	collective consciousness dispersed throught the division of labour
singular and absolute authority	authority functional and moderating
concrete cognitive structure meanings particularistic	abstract cognitive structure meanings universalistic and general
primary orientation for social action – altruistic	primary orientation for social action – egoistic
pervasive doctrines – conservative normative legal structure – repressive sanction	pervasive doctrines – innovative normative legal structure – restitutive sanction
form of control – positioned status-centred	form of control – personal, person-centred
experience of control – shame assigned social roles and status roles communalized weak boundary maintenance low discretion (public) individual experience of collective life through consensus symbolic systems – condensed correspondential symbols high communicative predictability	experience of control – guilt assigned social roles and status roles individualized strong boundary maintenance high level of discretion (private) individual experience of collective life through divergence symbolic systems – diffused, interpretive symbols low communicative predictability
low expression of unique intent speech mode – restricted FACT	high expression of unique intent speech mode – elaborated VALUE

order also legislates for the finite. The world is comprised of a fixed and limited number of segments and their possible relation – the model is, in Durkheim's own formulation, 'mechanical'. Society then, is intrinsically ordered, transcendently regulated and mechanistically maintained.

Such ruthless and unerring finitude has two epistemological consequences. First, the reduction of social phenomena to things, at hand, but not wilful nor independent. Such 'thing-like' status as derives from this shared, condensed symbolic order itself leads to the experience of phenomena in the constant, particularistic here-and-now of an unchanging cosmos. The second consequence is the reduction of the person, as a potential theorist. People within this form of life operate only on the surface, they are essentially irrelevant, except as a messenger; indeed, they too are relegated to the status of being one more 'thing' located mechanically within the true order of things, they have no 'intentional' relation with phenomena other than themselves.

The singular and absolute authority of the God that symbolizes mechanical solidarity ensures a unitary and necessarily shared epistemology. The strict rule system is worked out by taboo relating to the infringement of good conduct. The firm correspondence deriving from a restricted and condensed symbolic repertoire ensures only limited room for dissent – the same correspondential unequivocal symbols make for solidaristic and consensual group membership. The individual member, if indeed he or she is distinguishable as such, has only a positional responsibility to the rules of community, this emphasizes the reliance on one methodological way and further contributes to the weak sense of self – 'self as anyman' as McHugh (1971) puts it. In fact, such is the antipathy towards egoism within such a community that in methodological terms, 'self' becomes the source of all bias and corruption, as *The Rules of Sociological Method* (henceforth *Rules*) instructs us we must 'eliminate all preconceptions'.

Durkheim's Methodological Core

We can now view these methodological assertions in terms of Durkheim's early work, particularly the *Rules*. In the *Rules* the tone is prescriptive, it is as if Durkheim were legislating for the conduct of a scientific community. To suggest that such legislation be accompanied by repressive sanction would be to press the metaphor through analogy into simile; but the work is clearly 'laying down the laws' for the recognition

29

(ontology) and recovery (epistemology) of sociological phenomena and the rules are hardly stated in an equivocal or flexible fashion. The Preface begins with the tantalizing statement that:

> We are so little accustomed to treat social phenomena scientifically that certain of the propositions contained in this book may well surprise the reader. However, if there is to be a social science, we shall expect it not merely to paraphrase the traditional prejudices of the common man but to give us a new and different view of them; for the aim of all science is to make discoveries, and every discovery more of less disturbs accepted ideas. (Durkheim, 1964b: xxxvii)

So, we are promised a science of discoveries, and of surprises, and one capable of transcending common sense – and the *Rules* will enable us to achieve this end. The *Rules* has been variously described as a manifesto (Lukes, 1985; Thompson, 1982) in as much as it seeks to establish the rule system for a social science, but also in as much as it seeks to describe the nature of sociological phenomena. Of course, the character of this facticity is crucial. In what sense is it present, perhaps as a 'sign' and for Durkheim as a sign of different forms of relation both in-reality and in-thought? This, in turn, releases social phenomena from the epistemological imperialism of psychology, biology, individualist metaphysics and indeed, common sense. Thus, in this way, sociology's object is located, provided with a special identity and offered up for observation and understanding through a finite set of explicit transformational rules.

The primary entities that comprise a social world are social facts, they are the 'absolute simples', the irreducible elements that, in unique combinations, constitute different societal forms. Social facts are also the primary units of analysis. Durkheim seems at this stage to draw no distinction between objects of reality and objects of science, yet it is social science which releases such facts from their obscurity. The language of sociology brings this form of facticity into focus. The social facts are: 'every way of acting, fixed or not, capable of exercising on the individual an external constraint or again, every way of acting which is general throughout while at the same time existing in its own right independent of its individual manifestation' (ibid.: 13) and we are further instructed to 'consider social facts as things' (ibid.: 14).

The social facts, then, are typified through three major characteristics: externality, constraint and generality. They are *external* in the sense that they have an existence independent of our thought about them, they are not simply realized or materialized by the individual member and, further, they pre-date that member, and as such constitute any world that he or she enters. They *constrain* in as much as they are coercive when infringed; normal social conduct falls within their conventions and manifests their reality, attempts to act otherwise than normatively transgress the implicit and explicit rule structure and invoke constraint. Their *generality* derives from their being typical, normal, average, sustaining and not transitory, and morally good in the sense that they maintain the collective life – they are the very fabric of social 'nature' their generality enables them to speak for themselves, but through the auspices of sociological patronage; that is, they have a sociological facticity.

This last characteristic is further mobilized in Durkheim's method through the invocation that: 'The voluntary character of a practice or an institution should never be assumed beforehand' (ibid.: 28) which provides for the possibility that even the most arbitrary, isolated or seemingly random occurrence of a social phenomenon may, on further observation, be revealed to be yet a further necessary component within a systematic and stable social structure – indeed, the inherent order of things predicted in the 'mechanical' paradigm. These three characteristics of social facts would appear to be incompatible with the decidedly unstable and necessarily transitory nature of a subculture. Either a subculture is 'pathological' in Durkheim's sense (and what could be more pathological than a social bond based on 'style', for example?) or the concept provides a retreat position from which the theorist can account for the anomalous case.

Throughout this section of the text, where Durkheim is providing the rules for the observation of social facts, we could say that he is actually siting or locating the observer in such a manner that his perspective on reality cannot be other than that of a sociologist. Part of this siting involves instruction as to the extent of our observations but part also involves our insulation from all other viewpoints. Hence we are told: 'All preconceptions must be eradicated' (ibid.: 51). We must eschew the legitimacy of common sense as a starting point for social investigation. The obverse of this instruction is an implicit theory of the inadequacy or distorted character of pre-sociological speech, one which Durkheim makes clear with critical reference to biology, psychological reductions and to the categories of common sense itself. This points also to the mechanical sense of 'priest' or expert. For our purposes it would seem that Durkheim treats common sense as historically partial and thus prone to misrepresent the real, and so sociology, using the same sense agencies, but different categories to common sense, must serve to overcome this imaginary world. So here Durkheim is recommending a break away from the illusions of the subject and a systematic, 'disciplined' movement towards the real object. The production of common sense as distorted in this manner distances the social member from a lived, sensuous appreciation of the 'real' social world. There is a strong sense in which the member inevitably becomes relativized in the face of the preponderating finitude of the social, which is, as established, the primary reality. We must explain the social in terms of the social. This means that we should not resort to material or psychological reduction or confuse epiphenomena (such as subculture attempts to formulate) with the real object of our attention. The member, though integrated into the social and active in its reproduction through his or her day-to-day conduct, is unaware, analytically, of its true structure unless informed by the correct and singular rules of methodology. To adopt this method is, then, to attain a grasp of the real, thus it is the method and not the member that holds a constant and unerring relationship with the social; for the method to vary or to be person-based would give rise to a proliferation of realities, a secularization of Gods – an act of profanity. It is in this context, within the mechanical epistemology, that the individual, as theorist, is sensible beyond the surface only if he or she sublimates his or her difference to a corporate method and a singular reality.

Durkheim continues to inform us that social things are 'givens' and that they are subject to the practice of observation; this then becomes a central analytic problem, namely, to discover the rules that govern the visual existence of social things. We are given rules of recognition and assembly and we are to combine these rules with the social fact's proportions of thing-like-ness that we have already considered. So social facts are resistant to our individual will, our attempts to alter or amend them; they are objectively available, that is, free of possible interpretation or value judgement, and they are irreducible to other phenomena. They are, in terms of the social world, all that is the case. More than this, all manifestations of a social fact are linked by causality – the mechanical whole seems complete.

Recognition of the social facts remains, however, a problem. Although their existence is *sui generic*, they do not have form. Their reality does not consist in a material or physical presence, they are more experienced than tangible. Their manifestation is as constraint; they are invisible prison walls. Clearly they can be witnessed but only in a much as they inhabit or are realities – so Durkheim instances the legal system, the use of French currency, and the French language, all extant structural features embodying social facts. Ultimately, then, they are representations which arise from and are indicators of the collective consciousness – the methodological rules of the scientific community. It is interesting that within the mechanical paradigm the social facts constrain the individual and yet the social member remains largely non-theorized as an alternative causality. In a strong sense, the move to explanations in terms of subcultures is an attempt to liberate the individual 'intent' from this problematic, however, as an analytical move, it leaves the social unresolved.

The *Rules*, which marks out the character of the mechanical paradigm, produces science as a form of perception which has sensation as its basis. As, within this model, reality is viewed as an organized system with stable relations holding between the part and the whole, then also the relation between cause and effect is seen as logical rather than temporal – it is a fixed mechanical system and, as such, the model lent itself to a functionalist approach. From such a position the sociologist is concerned to observe the logical equilibrium of social systems, and comparisons are drawn through correspondences or homologies from one system to the next. Laws are established through the constant correspondence between variables within systems.

An important methodological distinction in the *Rules* is that made by Durkheim between the concepts of the *normal* and the *pathological*. He says that: 'for societies as for individuals, health is good and desirable; disease, on the contrary, is bad and to be avoided' (Durkheim, 1964b: 49) and also, in more general terms that: 'One cannot, without contradiction, even conceive of a species which would be incurably diseased in itself and by virtue of its fundamental constitution. The healthy constitutes the norm *par excellence* and can consequently be in no way abnormal' (ibid.: 58).

This crucial distinction then, refers to social facts that are typical and general (the normal) as opposed to those that are irregular, particular or transitory. It is useful distinction to exercise but we need to ask also why the concepts should have been employed, they would seem to operate at two levels. First and most obviously, at the concrete level of actual social members, the *normal* facts are those which constitute solidarity and continuity and the *pathological* are those which manifest individualization, fragmentation and interruption. In their different ways, the two orders of social fact are markers of good and concerted conduct within the collective life. Second, at the analytic level, and this is their main thrust, it might be suggested that the normal/pathological distinction is a moral distinction or election mode by the theorist in advance of his commitment to a programme of methodology. It is the theorist's projection of notions of choice and arbitration into the particular form of social structure that emanates from a mechanical form of life. The binary opposition contained within the normal/pathological distinction resembles the binary cognitive code necessary for the articulation of the individual and collective interests within a mechanical solidarity. Issues have to be resolved in absolutes of Yes and No, Collective and Individual. The lack of a developed division of labour disables the proliferation of views of justifiable positions. Thus, as the dialectic between normal and pathological facts can be seen to have a remedial and beneficial function at the concrete level of the social member, so also it has a function in the methodological social engineering of the theorist who seems to construct these facts as mechanically coherent.

Durkheim defines the normal in terms of the average, a definition which must continue to re-affirm itself – a sure feature of mechanical reproduction. The pathological elements are structurally transitory and thus inappropriate for our study; thus instead of using the concept 'pathological' to refer to inherent threats within a social structure Durkheim uses it to establish the asocial character of individual manifestations and through this to sanctify the altar of collective purity. Pathological behaviour serves as a negative reinforcement for the collective sentiments; crime creates outrage, punishment gives rise to expiation, the normal has its boundaries once more confirmed.

The average equates with the healthy which in turn equates with the good. Durkheim's method is clearly monotheistic in this particular model which is wholly appropriate for the structure of institutions and consciousness that it is, at one level, seeking to illuminate – namely primitive, simple, religiously based, coherent societies.

The next stage in Durkheim's methodology within the mechanical model involves the practice of classification. This activity aims at the construction of a social morphology – a scheme which distinguishes between yet logically relates what Durkheim refers to as social forms or social types. By adopting this middle range unit of analysis Durkheim hopes to avoid speaking in particularistic relativisms, on the one hand, or in gross a priori generalizations like 'humanity' or 'human nature', on the other. The social type, then, makes reference to a particular structuring of social relations; the simplest being the 'primitive horde', from which origins the forms progress in complexity through clans and tribes up until cities and states. As previously discussed, in relation to *The Division of Labour in Society* (henceforth *DoL*) all forms consist of the basic irreducible elements of social life that the 'horde' embodies, but they are distinguishable through their particular mode of aggregation of these elements. A classificatory scheme is thus to be achieved in terms of a series of definitions of modes of combination. The 'types' or 'species' are not seen as temporal stages, their systematic ordering is not evolutionary – they are logically synchronic not materially diachronic.

If we now regard the practice of classification as a metaphoric instance of the mechanical form of life, we find it wholly compatible with that model. The urge towards a strong system of classification is a desire to perpetuate order and firm control. To generate strong classification requires the election and maintenance of strong boundaries each marking off inflexible contents. In terms of social roles, strong boundaries enable static and secure identities to be exercised with a high degree of discretion. Within such a set of social relations there is little inter-dependency as each identity is self-sufficient and interactionally incapable of expressing need through difference. Strong classification instances the form of social relationships that precede the division of labour. Once again, the analytic of Durkheim's method is seen to reflect the concrete features of his simplest mode of solidarity.

The concluding stages of Durkheim's methodology in the mechanical model contained in the *Rules* proceed through explaining the newly classified social fact through seeking out: 'separately the efficient cause which produces it and the function it fulfils' (Durkheim, 1964b: 95).

The two important instances here with relation to the social fact are *cause* and *function*; within the mechanical model we might suggest that the former, *cause* which is constant and determinate, emanates from the intrinsic order of such a social world, it is like the word of God; the latter, *function*, is the word made man – it is man's practical, but nevertheless various and different, ways of enacting such a cosmic directive. Again, this process is metaphoric of the God-head in mechanical solidarity.

Finally, having moved from observation to theory, Durkheim's method within this model, finishes with the production of a general law; that is, a theory that will enable us to make predictive statements concerning the occurrence of the studied phenomenon in other social circumstances the ultimate act of control through reproduction.

The Move from the Semiotic to the Symbolic

Durkheim, with Marcel Mauss, introduces the problem of *Primitive Classification* (henceforth *PC*) with the statement that 'The discoveries of contemporary psychology have thrown into prominence the frequent illusion that we regard certain mental operations as simple and elementary when they are really very complex' (Durkheim and Mauss, 1970: 3).

Thus, we are aware of the ways that people relate to objects and states of affairs in the concrete world but we are little accustomed to treating our logical representations in discourse and consciousness as of the same nature. These, Durkheim states, we tend to treat as immanent in consciousness and refined through the history of experience and practice. So the conventional belief is that the capacity to classify and order the world is reducible to individual psychology – a belief that is coherent with the model of the typical actor contained within the society of the *Rules* – a naturalized unit responding to *sui generic* constraint. Durkheim notes, however, that within simple societies the capacity to differentiate between self and object or indeed between self and other appears to be absent, people may believe themselves to be like the crocodile, for example, and personality fuses into one continuous form. Thus, he suggests, in its origins, humanity 'lacks the most indispensable conditions for the classificatory function'. In its primal state humankind is ill-equipped to distinguish like from unlike and certainly unable to organize a ranking of things in hierarchical terms; the world as it presents itself to our observation does not display hierarchy – it is constructed as such.

Here we arrive at the central issue, if human cognition is not naturally endowed with the capabilities of constructing classifications, on what basis did such a systematic and regular occurring function develop? Durkheim seeks to reveal this basis in elementary social structures themselves. This fundamental relation between the social structure and the symbolic order renders highly problematic the proliferation of codes that would need to be established to demonstrate the 'social' nature of each subculture supposed to be at work. Rather what it suggests is that sociality transcends small group allegiance. To find one's identity in a segment of a classificatory system is to have at least a tacit knowledge of the whole of the classificatory system, not just the individual totem.

Durkheim and Mauss go on to demonstrate how systems of classification were generated and aim to specify the social forces that induce people to divide between classes. They employ second-order material, that is, speculative ethnographies concerning Australian Aborigines, North American Indians or Ancient Chinese communities. They point out that all such elementary societies appear to be sectioned into kinship groups which are intelligible as distinct in terms of the different expressions, forms and degrees of affective intensity contained within those various social relations. Of these social divisions, the largest and the oldest are termed 'moieties', these are the fundamental expressions of social affinity. Each moiety is further subdivided into 'clans' which proliferate into smaller marriage groups. These divisions, these expressions of belonging and relatedness are not capricious nor random, they relate directly to the style of relation encapsulated within them. In the explanation provided of how people in these structures perceive their world it is argued that all phenomena of the natural world, animate and inanimate, are seen to be treated as symbolically attributed to or belonging to particular specific groups, usually as totems. Initially this 'possession' is structured primarily in terms of the larger older groups (the moieties) and then subdivided more specifically into clans and smaller kinship associations. Durkheim and Mauss then liken this claiming of 'related' segments of the cosmos to our contemporary branching classificatory scheme. They suggest that, in concrete terms, through the mediating symbols of the totems, moieties provide for the original 'species' and the clans for the original 'genera'.

Durkheim and Mauss further argue that although modern scientific morphologies might appear to have become somewhat removed from their 'social origins', the very manner in which we still gather phenomena as 'belonging to the same family' reveals these social origins. Despite what they refer to as the acknowledged remove from primitive classifications up to the present day, Durkheim and Mauss wish to argue that primitive classifications are certainly not exceptional or singular. Rather, they assert, they are on a continuum, connected without a break in continuity up to the first scientific classifications. Indeed, 'primitive classifications' in themselves display the essential characteristics of all scientific classificatory systems, being that (i) they are arranged hierarchically, so that all phenomena of the natural world are perceived to be in a fixed relation with one another; and (ii) that they are speculative, in the sense that they are used for understanding or coming to terms with what is other than oneself.

Throughout his writings, Durkheim was concerned with the analytic problems of the successful establishment and appropriate interpretation of manifestations of the social bond. He worked at the production of a continuous morphology of possible rule systems by and through which people are oriented in their conduct, within, and as part of, the various orders that constitute society. He endeavoured, then, to construct the analytically conceived conditions for people living together; these would stand as the external organizing principles of society; and from this framework, it was stated their actions could be made intelligible in terms of that very living together. He was, at each level, concerned to explain the social in terms of the social. Thus, the later Durkheim sensitizes us to the centrality of symbolism in social life and now asserts that symbols themselves are fundamental in the structuring and interpretation of social experience.

Whereas the earlier work of the *Rules* revealed a mechanically explicit concern with the specification of the natural unequivocal moral order of society in terms of generalities, their constraining influence and thus their causal significance – the *sui generic* mechanistic reality – the later work of *Professional Ethics and Civic Morals* and *Elementary Forms of Religious Life* (henceforth *EFRL*) now shifts from the stance of a phenomenalistic positivism and directs itself to explain the non-observable, the non-material, the realms of mind, knowledge and symbolic representations; what Alexander (1988) has seen as the appropriate grounds for an analysis of culture. Substantively we move from institutions to beliefs, from laws and contracts to epistemologies and cosmologies – the latter Durkheim now uses as the occasion for his work, but he is also occasioned by them, they are part of his methodological purpose. When Durkheim begins to write his implicit epistemology, as a method, it reveals how a natural moral order is equivocally intelligible from within a complex interpretive network of diffuse symbols. The concerted or disciplined unification of understandings within this context points to the necessity and purpose of an organic method, a method that unites differences which are no longer identical, continuous or stable in their relations.

Durkheim is quite clear in his Introduction to *EFRL* that he is involved in an analysis of totemism, in the first instance, as a critical illumination of his general theory of religion; this, however, is in turn only one facet of his wider theory of knowledge, the culmination of all his studies. It is, then, the epistemology that is his principal, underlying concern throughout the study, and religion may be conceptualized as relating to the symbolic system through which man addresses his world and through which his world and his consciousness are constructed. The importance of religious theory goes far beyond an examination of the social character of ceremony or ritual – it indicates the very nature of human knowledge. So, for Durkheim, religion sheds light not only on what people believe but more fundamentally in what and on how they think.

The substantive truth value of elements comprising a mechanical order is attested to by Durkheim in the Introduction to the *EFRL* when he states that there exist in society no institutions that are based upon a lie. Within a positivist world all phenomena are present to us and coherent by virtue of their ultimate reality, the symbol and its referent are as one. Thus, all religious practice, whatever form it takes, translates some human need. Religions embody a specific social function which is their recognizable constraint.

Durkheim's concern with the origins of symbolism is made paramount in his discussion of the 'categories of understanding', that is, the ultimate principles which underlie all our knowledge and which give order and arrangement to our perceptions and sensations, thus enabling us 'to know' at all. He wishes to establish the social derivation of these basic categories such as, for example, concepts of space, time, class, substance, force, efficacy, causality etc. – all concepts which were taken to be universally valid fundamentals of all human thought:

> Instead of Durkheim's saying 'the unconscious is history', one could write 'the a priori is history'. Only if one were to mobilize all the resources of the social sciences would one be able to accomplish this kind of historicist actualization of the transcendental project which consists of reappropriating, through historical anamnesis, the product of the entire historical operation of which consciousness too is (at every moment) the product. In the individual case this would include reappropriating the dispositions and classificatory schemes which are a necessary part of the aesthetic experience as it is described, naively, by the analysis of essence. (Bourdieu, 1993: 256)

Reviewing the dominant epistemological explanations Durkheim dismisses the types of idealism which depict the ultimate reality behind the world as being spiritual, informed by an Absolute; or those which account for the categories as being inherent in the nature of human consciousness. Such an 'a priorist' position, he says, is refuted by the incessant 'variability' of the categories of human thought from society to society; and, further, it lacks experimental control, it is not empirically verifiable. Indeed, such a position 'does not satisfy the conditions demanded of a scientific hypothesis'. In this section he can be read as addressing the Kantian edifice which has a theory of mind as that being informed by divine reason. For Kant the categories exist somehow beyond the individual consciousness as prior conditions of experience and without which experience would be meaningless and chaotic – the divine reason is thus made manifest through individual consciousness.

Durkheim also criticizes the varieties of subjectivism, in particular the theory stating that individuals construct the categories from the raw materials of their own particular empirical experience or perception; that is, we each infer and create our own unique set of categories from the peculiar orderings of our own sensations. This is the extreme logical position of the tradition of empiricism, and in this context Durkheim is addressing the anthropology of Tylor and Frazer. Durkheim suggests that although the categories of thought vary from society to society, within any one society they are characterized by universality and necessity. Thus, for the subjectivists, since all sensations are private, individual and different, it is difficult in terms of their theory to account for how people generally come to possess and operate with the same categories within particular societies. This is an important reflection on the potential isolationism inherent in subcultural theory.

Durkheim also, at this stage of his work, dissociates himself from any materialist standpoint. In order to avoid deriving mind from matter, or invoking any supra-experiential reality Durkheim says that it 'is no longer necessary to go beyond experience' – and the specific experience to which he is referring is the 'super-individual reality that we experience in society'. He considers that people do not make the world in their own conscious image any more than that the world has imposed itself upon them, indeed, 'they have done both at the same time'. Although within the *EFRL*, he makes occasional reference to 'objectivities' and to 'the nature of things', he continues to speak throughout to a 'super-individual reality' which is not the material world – it is society as a symbolic universe.

For Durkheim, society is the fundamental and primary reality; without it there is no humankind – but this is a reciprocal dependency. Society can only be realized, can only become conscious of itself and thus make its influence felt through the collective behaviour of its members, that is, through their capacity to communicate symbolically. From this concerted conduct springs the collective representations and sentiments of society and further, the fundamental categories of thought, for they too are collective representations. Thus, humankind finds expression only in and through the social bond; and, of course, this bond is itself an expression of sociology's epistemology:

Anthropology and in particular Durkheim in the Année Sociologique group developed a tradition that is continued in the structuralism of Lévi-Strauss. And while Bourdieu takes issue with the Durkheimian model, the social determinism that works via the formation of individual habitus indicates a continued fascination with what might be called Kantian subjectivity, and with the social bases of cultural classification. Certainly, the generation of schemes of classification and of social distinction in the practice of social relations is an essential ingredient in the formation of social and individual identity. (Lash and Friedman, 1992: 4)

The movement from the early to the late Durkheim depicts a move from form to content. The *Rules* instances a firm positing of society as a concrete reality and implies an abstract and implicit concept of the person within this model, man as consciousness emerges as an epiphenomenon of society. In the place of a member's consciousness the *Rules* substitutes collective responses to constraint. Such positivism sets a strict limit to human understanding and creativity – the limit being not merely the isolated individual's sense impression, but the sense impressions of the individual as a compelled member of a unified collective consciousness. The collective consciousness is thus the teleological representation the ultimate and finite reality structure.

In the later Durkheim symbolism is produced as fundamental to cultural formation, it can give rise to the self as potentially analogous to society but also as potentially different from that society. Thus, symbolism is consciously creative, its occurrence and its interpretation, both by lay members of particular forms of society and by Durkheim as the methodological architect of these different forms of understanding, distance the sign from the signified. The capacity to symbolize opens up the distinction between objects-in-thought and objects-in-reality which were conflated in Durkheim's early realist epistemology. The content of the person is now imbued with potential and choice. Durkheim articulates this sense of diffusion between the collective and the individual representations through his concepts of the 'sacred' and 'profane'. Initially, the presence of sacred things provides a substantive criterion for the existence of religion. Sacredness, then, denotes religiosity.

At another level, this common characteristic of all religious belief, namely, the recognition of the sacred and the profane presupposes a classification of all things, actual and imaginary, into two opposing domains. The two realms are not alternatives, they are profoundly distinct, ranked in terms of power and dignity, and insulated by antagonism and hostility. 'The sacred is *par excellence* that which the profane should not touch, and cannot touch with impunity' (Durkheim, 1971: 40). The two orders jealously patrol their own boundaries to prevent the contamination of one by the other and thus the perpetually revivified structure of interdictions or taboos, serves to keep things apart. Transition from one realm to the other is not wholly precluded, but it requires not movement but metamorphosis.

At yet a further level Durkheim's notions of the sacred and the profane reflect the experiential tension between the social interest and the personal interest. The sacred may be seen to represent public knowledge and social institutions, and the profane represents the potential of individual consciousness, it is that which is always threatening to bring down the sacred; it is that which, in Mary Douglas's (1966) terms, promises 'danger'. The bifurcation of human interests provided for by these deep structural binaries, reveals the grounds of the epistemological differences between the mechanical positivism of the early Durkheim and the organic hermeneutic of the late Durkheim, and these grounds are moral. What could possibly produce the sentimental experience of the sacred through the febrile attachment provided by a subculture?:

> Douglas selected for inclusion a part of Herz's book on the hand ... in which he argues that the distinction between right- and left-handedness concerns the sacred and the profane. He saw this as a widespread distinction that could not be explained in terms of 'nature'. He did not deny that there were physical differences between the two sides of the body, he only denied that such differences explained the consistency with which diverse cultures affirm the priority of the right hand. Herz's interest in the hand derived from the fact that it stood for an abstract principle – the sacred and the profane must be kept separate and their relationship strictly controlled for the sake of (a sense of) order. (Jordanova, 1994: 253)

The early work proceeds from compact, continuous symbols. Such symbols occur as social facts which are contingent upon mechanical perception, we feel their constraint, we observe their presence. Their sacredness derives from their reification (or substantively their deification) into constant components of a consensus world view, this characterizes the method; it emanates from close, shared, uncritical communities of thinkers – its moral imperative is a demand for obligation, a membership of unquestioning allegiance.

The later Durkheim takes up a concern with the potency of diffused, fragmented symbols. This is a symbolic universe potentially populated by varieties of egoism. Within such a model all shifts towards the ascendance of the individual over the collective threaten to produce a crisis in our classificatory systems – a deregulation, a condition already predicted in *DoL* as 'anomie'. With reference to primitive religion Durkheim shows us in the *EFRL* that a 'totem' is identified with an object of nature and thus produces it as different and knowable, that is, as having boundaries. The totem is in itself symbolic of the social group that produced it as a totem. Thus, proliferating groups within any social structure 'objectify themselves' in material objects as totems; the totem then acts as an emblem which the member identifies with and thus, through identification, remains part of his group. Elementary methodic practices, like ritual, can now be seen to involve the periodic celebration and renewal of collective sentiments, by way of the symbolic totem.

The impact of the study of totemic religion on Durkheim's later epistemology, then, is that totems seem to demonstrate the beginnings of understanding. Totems are not the things themselves, they stand for or in the place of things and forms of relationship – in this sense they are metaphoric. Thus they instance a break from the continuity provided by compact symbols between material reality and consciousness, they act as a mediating order whose status derives from the work of interpretation. Totems, then, belong to difference, in that they require the individual to relate to them as something other than they manifestly are; totems also are derived from difference in that they are brought into being through an elementary affective division of labour. In both these ways totems are potentially profane, that is, they most forcefully give rise to the tension between consensus understanding and belief, and individual interpretation. To live in a world of diffused symbols but to share that world requires an organic epistemology, it requires self-conscious discipline and commitment, not a sense of obligation of allegiance.

The organic epistemology rests on the distinction between the sign and the referent; things are not as they appear. Their appearance is contingent upon intentionality which is saved from animism through a theoretical commitment to a principled way of formulating the world. This is the community experience of the shared totem of an elected tradition. The constraint inherent in the positivistic mechanical model, comprised of 'sui generic' and the spatialized consciousness, now requires individual representation. The organic form of life is ordered, as it is social, but its order derives not from determinism but from interpretation and reflexivity. It presents itself reflexively as a formulation which is open to and available for reflexive formulations. The disciplined character of this new way of realizing the world depends not on obedience to external methodological rules but on a thoughtful explication of grounds – its availability. This subtle normative order may be likened to the experiential constraint of taboo, but the sacred writ is no longer clear to us, as Durkheim has told us: 'the old gods are growing old or already dead, and others are not yet born; it is life itself, and not a dead past which can produce a living cult' (1971: 427).

The rules are no longer clear and we are freer because of this, our responsibility, however, is to constitute the social world and to believe in those constitutions for, as Durkheim says, we can no longer receive the world from closed systems of knowledge: 'for faith is before all else an impetus to action, while science, no matter how far it may be pushed, always remains at a distance from this. Science is fragmentary and incomplete; it advances but slowly and is never finished; but life cannot wait' (ibid.: 431).

That 'life cannot wait' is sufficient as grounds and manifesto for the emergent late-modern sociologist. Durkheim's thesis was no absolutist triumph over the will, his dual ways of being provided inspiration and fortitude in the face of modern and late-modern tendencies to blur and distort both the boundary and the category contained, through such devices as subculture.

Guilds and Workgroups as Proto-Subcultures

In *Professional Ethics and Civic Morals* Durkheim comes closest to constituting the elementary forms of subcultures but also salvages the situation by recognizing the necessity of adopting a conservative rather than individualistic solution. The problem is that society, forms of solidarity, have seemingly not kept pace with the speed of social change. As we put it earlier, the categories of a modernist sociology no longer adequately attach to the everyday experience of individuals and their new-found experience of group or multi-group attachment. This is in large part due to the gap that has formed between the involuntary, sentimental attachment we feel for primary groups and the elective and instrumental attachment we chose in relation to the public sphere. In the late-modern society the latter is symbolized through the free market and its spiralling, unprincipled detachment from all forms of human association – this is not a meeting place governed by any internal or systematic moral bond. Now the postmodern response to such conditions is an expression of liberation and the realization of a new multi-faceted identity sited in subcultures bound by fashion, lifestyle, consumption, logo, style, populist aesthetics and ego-indulgence sometimes acknowledged as unconscious political resistance.

For Durkheim, this collapse into mannerism and abandonment of cohesion is far from an option. Durkheim sees the solution to a generally recognized concern (but variously perceived as desirable or threateningly undesirable) as one of describing human mechanisms through which control will be restored. Durkheim recommends the development of structures of professional codes and civic ethics, previously upheld by guilds and workgroups to keep the medieval economy in check, to regulate the modern market. The benign modern state should police the regulation of the organic solidarity by soliciting the support of a range of professional mechanical micro-solidarities and engendering a new civic morality of altruism (albeit cognitive rather than affective):

> No regulated planning means no regularity ... the more the dimensions of societies increase and the more markets expand, the greater the urgency of some regulation to put an end to this instability. Because, as discussed earlier, the more the whole exceeds the part, the more the society extends beyond the individual, the less can the individual sense within himself the social needs and social interests he is bound to take into account.
>
> Now, if these professional ethics are to become established in the economic order, then the professional group, hardly to be found in this sphere of social life, must be formed or revived. For it is this group alone that can work out a scheme of rules ... The name in history of this professional group is the guild. (Durkheim, 1992: 17)

Max Weber: Groups Bound by Reason and Authority

Interestingly enough Max Weber's (1864–1920) contribution to our current debate concerning the classical origins and obviations of subcultural thinking is neither major nor startlingly original. In *The Theory of Social and Economic Organization* he discusses types of solidarity and social relationships. He draws a distinction between *communial* and *associative* relationships which he defines as follows:

> A social relationship will be called 'communial' if and so far as the orientation of social action ... is based on a subjective feeling of the parties, whether affectual or traditional, that they belong together ... The purest

cases of associative relationship are: (a) rational free market exchange, which constitutes a compromise of opposed but complementary interests; (b) the pure voluntary association based on self-interest, a case of agreement as to a long-run course of action oriented purely to the promotion of specific ulterior interests, economic or other, of its members; (c) the voluntary association of individuals motivated by an adherence to a common set of values. (Weber, 1964: 136)

And Weber describes these two forms as *Vergemeinschaft* and *Vergesellschaft* and acknowledges his debt to Tönnies, whom we have previously discussed. His criteria for the constitution of a social relationship are quite fierce and he dismisses ethnicity, shared language and a shared symbolic repertoire as in themselves sufficient. He invokes a notion of belonging which is resonant with Durkheim's social bond. He then considers openness and closure in social relationships and states that closure does not constitute a relationship but it does constitute 'membership' which may tentatively approach the mode of association gathered as subculture. Membership and belonging make reference to more surface characteristics as insignia and practice rather than need or desire. Bad deeds, attitude, dressing, dancing and consumption appear to be the most explicit motifs of subculture. Membership of criminal subcultures is a sign of fallenness, 'nobody else would have me', the melancholic conclusion to Becker's (1963) saga on 'Becoming a Marihuana User' is 'I knew I was really hooked when all my friends were junkies' – not really the basis for either a cognitive or affective social contract. Alternatively more modern 'youth' subcultural studies seem to revolve around 'opting in', being a member of the in-crowd, mob, gang, tribe, trend, clique, fashion movement – again, hardly striking manifestations of an instrumental rationality.

Similarly, none of Weber's three forms of group-binding authority seems to apply to the case that is subculture, they are neither *rational* in terms of using the most appropriate means to achieve the most appropriate ends, nor *traditional* in terms of the affectual demands for conformity. Subcultures slenderly approximate to the mode of *charisma* but in a disembodied form and then only as charisma routinized:

In its pure form charismatic authority has a character specifically foreign to everyday routine structures. The social relationships directly involved are strictly personal, based on the validity and practice of charismatic personal qualities. If this is not to remain a purely transitory phenomenon, but to take the character of a permanent relationship forming a stable community of disciples ... it is necessary for the character of charismatic authority to become radically changed...It cannot remain stable but becomes either traditionalized or rationalized, or a combination of both. (Weber, 1964: 363–4)

Marx: the *Lumpenproletariat*

Finally, what has Karl Marx (1818–83) to add to our debate? This is not meant to pre-empt our discussions of the neo-Marxist ideas of hegemony, interpellation and ideological state apparatuses reworked through the ideas of the Birmingham School and considered more fully in Chapter 6. Do we find anything in Marx's total corpus of work that might help us in our adventure towards understanding the origins, point and need for the concept of subculture? Well, possibly.

In a sense, previously alluded to, the idea of a subculture sometimes evolves into theory as a way of assembling the lost, rejected, the fallen, or perhaps more analytically those excluded by the dominant, normative classificatory structure of relationships in society. This is very much the resonance intended through the notion of 'deviant' or 'criminal' subculture. Although, in reality, such groupings may offer marginal exchange in the form of support, tutelage, continuity or role model they are, in effect, assemblages of the outcast, the unaccountable, those excluded by previous theories of solidarity. Marx has written, not altogether sympathetically, about precisely such clusterings in the wake of capitalism and in the advance towards revolution. Herewith, we find Marx's concept of the *Lumpenproletariat*, the 'dangerous class' that has dropped through the safety net of active consciousness or even an identity through labour attachment. He speaks of them thus: 'The "dangerous class", the social scum, that passively rotting mass thrown off by the lowest layers of old society, may, here and there, be swept into the movement by a proletarian revolution; its conditions of life, however, prepare it far more for the part of a bribed tool of reactionary intrigue' (Marx, quoted in McLellan, 1988: 29), and at one elevation:

> The lowest sediment of the relative surplus population finally dwells in the sphere of pauperism. Exclusive of vagabonds, criminals, prostitutes, in a word the 'dangerous' classes, this layer of society consists of three categories. First, those able to work. One need only glance superficially at the statistics of English pauperism to find that the quantity of pauperism increases with every crisis, and diminishes with every revival of trade. Second, orphans and pauper children. These are candidates for the industrial reserve army, and are, at times of great prosperity, as 1860, speedily and in large numbers enrolled in an active army of labourers.

Third, the demoralised and ragged, and those unable to work, chiefly people who succumb to their incapacity for adaptation, due to the division of labour ... Pauperism is the hospital of the active-labour army and the dead weight of the industrial reserve army ... pauperism forms a condition of capitalist production ... It enters into the *faux frais* (unnecessary expenditure) of capitalist production; but capitalism knows how to throw these, for the most part, from its own shoulders onto those of the working class and the lower middle class. (Marx, quoted in McLellan, 1988: 53–4)

This is the sad side of Marx. If we stretch his thesis, we might find more positive manifestations of micro-solidarity formations (i.e. subcultural formation) in his ideas on the development of a revolutionary class. For Marx, whatever the experiential character of capitalist society, the real sets of relations between people are always masked or mystified behind a smokescreen of ideology. Thus, however the individual may experience his or her sense of worth, belonging, solidarity or identification with a wider society, there is always a gulf, a divide and a schism determined by the actual material relations between people. Primarily, and indisputably for Marx, the advent and advance of capitalism force, through the division of labour, a critical stratification between people. This formative stratification is based on the ownership of the means of production – quite simply, some people do, and the others, of necessity, service those means of production and thus work for and are subservient towards those who do. This fundamental fracture in whatever previously established conventions that existed for people living together, bifurcates the society in a manner that is irresolvable through natural process. The division is lasting and antagonistic, its analytical roots are to be found in Hegel and thus it is realized as an antipathy, a negation, a remoulding of the master–slave dichotomy of mentalities, an historical struggle for recognition and, it follows, the perfect setting for a revolutionary dialectic. Now, in its unconscious condition, such a capitalist society gets by with a semblance of solidarity because of a whole series of ideological beliefs and infrastructural systems that convince all members that the going order is meant to be and based on natural (or even supernatural) divisions, even though it is clearly only one group that benefits from such a system. The beneficiaries, the *bourgeoisie*, the owners of the means of production, manage the disposed, the *proletariat*, either through oppression or through patrician means, but they manage them and thus contain the dissent, exploitation and manifest material differences in lifestyle. The material differences are maintained through a simple and inexorable feature of capitalist economies, namely profit. The proletariat work for themselves for part of their day but their labour power accrues a value that is greater than that which it earns, this is called surplus value and is the very source of profit. Of course, within this sociological treatise rather than within the terms of its political economy, the concept of surplus value disguises the real relationship between people, which is one of exploitation, accepted as natural by all within the conventions of a capitalist society. Now Marx's message is moral and it is revolutionary because it is imploring people to consider their conditions in non-'normative' and unacceptable ways. Once they slough off the false consciousness that is holding them suspended in antagonism and exploitative misery, then they will enjoy the real possibility of a new form of social structure where stratifications are dispensed with. The 'revolutionary' step towards true consciousness requires a deconstruction of the going order, a disassembly of the known forms of solidarity and the development of a new form of solidarity that is based peculiarly on class interest. This movement from darkness into light, from misapprehension into truth and clarity, from being merely a class-in-itself to becoming a class-for-itself involves the dissolution of social structures as we know them and the purposive generation of a new critical subculture of change and praxis. A class-for-itself 'might' be seen as an elemental subculture, it is a will to alternative solidarity, it is a consciously sought-after social bond. The reader might here consider the *glissade* from a European communist revolutionary class to Hebdige's (1979) mods and rockers just too much to take on, especially when the latter were mostly supposed to be unconscious of the political resistance that they offered, however, the continuum is available in analytical terms.

THREE The Missing Narrative I
The Chicago School

> What exactly is, or was, the Chicago school? Was it a group of people or a set of ideas? Was it a brief moment or a long-running tradition? Was it produced by a confluence of larger forces or by the force of individual personalities ... the Chicago school wasn't a thing at all, but rather a way of becoming a thing ... [it] ... was not a thing, a fixed arrangement of social relationships or intellectual ideas that obtained at a given time. It was rather a tradition of such relationships and ideas combined with a conception of how that tradition should be reproduced over time. (Abbott, 1999: 1)

Chicago and the sociology of Chicago combine to make up an extraordinary phenomenon. This is a vertical city built on a delta that empties into a lake the size of a sea. The city knows only two seasons, summer and winter, there are no gradients like spring and fall, the boundaries mark out major differences. The grid system on which the city was planned and built is equally clear in its pattern of differentiation, corners are sharp and square and there is no confusion about the urban geography, East 22nd Street is where it should be. As if to mimic, rather than mock, this architectural regimentation the incredibly diverse population assumed a symbolic grid and sought to insulate its identities and differences from one another. That the early Chicago urban sociology adopted an ecological model that would map the zones of 'Little Sicily', 'the Loop', 'Deutschland', 'China Town', 'the Ghetto', and so on, was neither inaccurate nor a flight of fancy. Beyond this the social mosaic policed its cracks to prevent them becoming joins and the sociology reflected this 'edge' in the city and the demarcations as contributing to social control. Mass immigration of widely disparate ethnicities, conflict, violence, organized crime, low life, poverty and corruption all contributed to the complex. Chicago certainly vied with New York for first city status. Chicago sociology has iterated through a number of forms yet certain elements remain constant and provide for its easy identification. The concept of a subculture will eventually emerge as an integral and inevitable element.

W.I. Thomas held the first ever Chair of Sociology at the University of Chicago, in one sense, his appointment in the late nineteenth century professionalized the discipline. Thomas was Professor of Sociology even before Durkheim and this marked out an independence. Whereas East Coast American sociology, mostly at Harvard and New York, adopted the mantle of the European classical tradition (and most specifically the French tradition), Chicago remained aloof and would have attached more allegiance to Gabriel Tarde's psychology of the crowd than to Durkheim's *sui generis* society and collective consciousness. Chicago sociology was much more person-centred, more individualistic, micro, or what has come to be formulated as social-psychological. Even when the work seemed most preoccupied with issues of urban sociology, it could have been described as interactionist and this would have been a designation acceptable to such as Robert Park and Ernest Burgess.

The Self in Interaction

Instead of viewing people as if they were constantly determined and prey to the constraint of external factors in this tradition, we find the individual actor occupying central stage. This factor is heavily emphasized within the theory, the social actor is treated not as a 'puppet' but as a 'Self'. From this framework the practice of becoming, of socialization, of the passage of social life itself, takes on a very different significance. Rather than being seen as a necessary, but deflecting, process 'becoming' is regarded as absolutely central to the interactionists' concerns, and far from being regarded as a transitory stage or a once-and-for-all process, it is seen rather as a perpetual and self-renewing process within social life. We might go as far as to say that 'becoming' provided the interactionists with a primary metaphor through which to begin explaining social life itself. The individual is considered to be routinely and yet regularly engaged in the practice of engaging in new and challenging interactional situations and thus learning as he or she lives. The dual ideas that socialization is 'on-going' or 'life-long', and also that the point of continuous interactional exchanges is to successfully negotiate their outcome with other actors point to the twin philosophical origins of symbolic interactionism itself, being 'evolutionism' and 'pragmatism'. Evolutionism is a form of optimistic humanism that interweaves the notions of change, growth and progress and produces a moral account of history. Pragmatism, when first developed by Charles Pierce, was a philosophy of meaning asserting that the idea of the sense effects of an object is the whole of the idea of the object. Pragmatism was further developed by William James into a theory of truth which held that an idea is true if it works satisfactorily, that is, it produces anticipated experiences for the actor. The conceptualization of socialization as being a continuous or life-long process has given rise to what the interactionists call 'adult socialization' – this is one of their central concepts which appears in many of their studies, particularly their studies of occupations.

The origins of the Chicago symbolic interactionist tradition are to be found in a variety of sources. Of particular significance are the early works of Charles Cooley, William Thomas and James Baldwin in the USA. Independently, inspiration was found in the micro-sociology of Georg Simmel, who published often in the *American Journal of Sociology* (a University of Chicago publication inaugurated by Albion Small, the first Sociology Head of Department), and also, and less directly, in Max Weber's rational '*Verstehen*' sociology from Germany. Clearly, however, the most significant and comprehensive formulation of the position, in the explicit form of symbolic interactionism, is to be found in the collected papers of the American social psychologist George Herbert Mead, the collection appearing under the title of *Mind, Self and Society* (1934). This body of thought has given rise to the large and flourishing American tradition of symbolic interactionism spreading mostly through the research and teaching of a group of scholars working in the faculty of sociology at the University of Chicago. The early period, up to the Second World War, witnessed the presence of Robert Park, Ernest Burgess, Ellsworth Faris and William Thomas; from their supervision emerged such figures as Everett C. Hughes, Herbert Blumer, Louis Firth, Paul Cressey and Clifford Shaw. A more recent generation of scholars would include Howard Becker, Anselm Strauss, Erving Goffman, Blanche Geer, Arnold Rose and Julius Roth. It would be hard not to concede the quality, inspiration and influence emanating from this 'hall of fame'.

Clearly, this group of people engaged in a whole range of sociological work, not all of which can be fitted within a convenient definition of sense of paradigm, however, Abbott puts it succinctly when he says:

The work these people produced falls under no simple characterization or single paradigm. There is, however, a typical stance to it, one that sets it apart from other sociological work at the time ... It is often about the city and, if so, nearly always about Chicago. It is processual – examining organization and disorganization, conflict and accommodation, social movements and cultural change. It imagines society in terms of groups and interaction rather than in terms of individuals with varying character-istics. Methodologically it is quite diverse, but it always has a certain empirical, even observational character ...

In retrospect, the work can be seen to have some clear emphases. Some of these were conceptual, like the tradition's interest in the link between individual and group 'minds,' the problem it called 'social psy-chology.' Others were empirical, like the intensive focus of the city. Still others were theoretical, like the idea of ecology. But none of these emphases was absolute. It was rather a stance of investigation, the inten-sity of commitment, and the structural and processual vision – if anything – that made the Chicago school a 'real' cultural unit. (Abbott, 1999: 6)

Symbolic Interaction as Social Psychology

It is important, for the argument to be developed here in relation to the idea of a 'subculture' that we dwell on the issue of symbolic interac-tion as social psychology. If we look, for a moment, at the major emphasis put on the generative power of the self, the actor. This tradi-tion argued most forcefully concerning the centrality and the absolute uniqueness of human behaviour. At another level they also systemat-ically advised that the key to understanding society as a whole lay in a detailed understanding of the typical features of individual human action. So, as was also the case for Weber, the prime concern of soci-ological, or socio-psychological, investigation is the explanation of meaningful social behaviour. This meaningful behaviour – meaningful in the sense of being intentional or having a purpose – is what has come to be properly referred to as 'social action'. What sociologists within an interpretative paradigm have come to mean by social action is human conduct that has a subjective meaning, indeed a motive, for the individual actor.

Resting on this assumption, a sense of rationality within human conduct is supposed to be active, interactive, creative and, indeed, what Garfinkel would later describe as artful. Social actors think about their concerns, problems, values or needs and then act in ways that they consider the best to achieve the ends that they have appointed themselves. So, in the context of this tradition of theorizing, we are not talking about animal instinct or stimulus-response knee-jerk reactions, this is not mere 'behaviour' but human, rational action. This self-conscious rationality, within symbolic interaction, is both descriptive of human action but also a continuous and developing feature of that action itself. So the reason develops with the interactional practice and each reflects back on the other. So, unlike in the Parsonian model that we shall consider in the next chapter, within this perspective individuals are not conceptualized as docile and obedient objects that are merely reacting under constraint. On the contrary, what we are offered here is an overwhelming concern with human decision-making and human purpose. Indeed, a major part of the sociological analysis that follows within symbolic interactionism is concerned with an articulation of those practices of decision-making. Within this active and interpretative perspective what is paramount is the idea of conscious, thinking subjects, actually planning and carrying out courses of action. We could say that unlike in the world of structural or systems sociology, where people are supposed to live in a symbolic environment ordered and controlled by material forms and objectivities, here the subjective dimension is avowedly in the ascendant.

Within symbolic interactionism our theoretical attention is directed away from a concern with global explanations to local explanations, from generalities to particularities, from social totalities or structures to individuals. To put it another way, we could say that we theorists should eschew the monolithic structures or systems which were supposed to determine the lives of the puppets or prisoners who supposedly populated them. We should cease to construct what Harold Garfinkel has referred to as 'cultural dopes', that is actors who are apparently directed by the rules of a society that they do not seemingly understand. And we can turn our backs on what Ralph Dahrendorf has described as 'homo sociologicus', that is an actor who is essentially comprised of the bundle of role-expectations that the sociologist has projected onto him. Now these supposed liberations, both analytic and concrete, appear to have a great appeal. They are also the source of a great deal of criticism of the interactionists' work. To ignore the structural, the global and the general is to leave it intact. To ignore this more macro-level of analysis is to skip over critical social issues like the distribution of power and resources in society. Marxist commentators, such as C. Wright Mills, have pointed out that the capitalist base of modern America is simply accepted as the backdrop to all subsequent interactionist studies. And this is a flaw in micro, socio-psychological analysis that conventional sociology has fought to overcome. We need to make 'why' statements about social structures, we need to know if the interactional sequence we are investigating is taking place within a liberal or a totalitarian regime, and whether all members of the interactional sequence are differently endowed with power. Do the policemen and the juvenile delinquents that we meet in the accounts of Chicagoan subcultures live suspended in a democratic harmony? Of course not. Perhaps then, we might assume that the typifications, the social reactions and the labels that figure so significantly in symbolic interactionists' studies are possible at all because of power differentials. The very set of social problems that the Chicago School spent so much of their century of investigating are 'problems' in the first place because of the nature of the social structure. The intense relationship between the transitory laws regarding Prohibition and the growth of organized crime should have been instructive in this regard. Nevertheless, the overall message is clear, within the interactionists' model of the actor, explanations tend to veer away from unidirectional causality, from the singular determinism and inevitable reductionism of structural sociology. The world stands still, the social structure is taken as a constant variable.

Symbolic interactionism, therefore, directs us to address individual actors, but not individuals in isolation as this is a sociological not a psychological theory. Individuals are our topic but individuals as they relate to one another in the process of interaction. More specifically we might say that the source of interest for interactionism is individuals united in an intersubjective web or network of meaning – this is a much looser, more fluid and potentially changeable concept than that of a social structure. We are engaged in a perspective primarily concerned with individual human choice and decision-making, we might therefore anticipate that any social phenomenon, indeed any social situation, will have potentially different meaning and significance for different individuals. That is, we can anticipate that different actors' interpretations of a situation will vary for a whole spectrum of reasons such as, for example, their value systems, their belief systems, their age, their gender, their class, their nationality, their education, their interests or even according to where they are standing. The sociality of these different individuals resides in the symbolism, the shared signs or meanings, that contrives to unite them within a more or less coherent definition of the situation of which they are a part.

We might say that the interactionists would argue that to generalize about the constituent features of a society's social structure, such as, for example, its educational system, its occupational system, its system of stratification, and so on, in the way that structural-functionalism or systems theory would, is to ignore the basic face-to-face mechanisms of social life. In other words, abstract talk and theorizing about systems and structures fail to recognize the startlingly obvious fact that people practically, or concretely, construct meaningful worlds on a person-to-person, day-to-day basis. Structural sociology fails to recognize or pay sufficient attention to the significance and importance of ordinary everyday people's ability to attach symbolic meanings to things in their world, to other people in their world, and to the action of themselves and other people in that world. The interactionists' perspective seeks an understanding of the basis of social organization in people's obvious and perceived capacity to manage and control their own circumstances. Any individual, or social actor, demonstrates his or her ability to exercise control by the way in which they assess a situation and then place a definition upon that situation. This is not usually a wholly wilful or capricious activity, we cannot choose to define a block of flats as a banana, but some propagandists might have us believe that a dictatorship is a democracy. The point here is that there are certain social conventions, red lights are always perceived as red and therefore indicating warning or stop, but within and also beyond these conventions people are very powerful in controlling and defining their particular situation.

The Social Context of Meaning

Max Weber, in his essays on sociological method, says that the world could be almost anything, it is infinite in its possibilities, but human beings ensure that it is always something and thus produce its stability by defining it and thus exercising control over it. Therefore, by defining a situation, an actor generates his or her own possibilities, and, by thus defining, that same actor is also exercising control and creating and reproducing the social conditions of control in interaction with other actors.

Meaning, from the interactionists' perspective, derives from interpersonal interaction, and it is from this context that the experience of social life as orderly also derives. Actors are not constrained by the search for meaning and thus order at the level of social structure. Actors are not visualized as guessing, or aspiring towards, or acting as automatons in relation to central values or societal norms. In as much as such standards exist, they are treated as emerging out of the negotiation and agreement that occur within interaction. Actors, then, are given the responsibility and autonomy of acting according to their own understanding of social life, they are not treated as pawns within a theorist's structural framework. As we have previously stated, within the context of conventional sociological terminology, the level of analysis has shifted from the 'macro' to the 'micro', and from the supposed and unavailable to the actual and the available.

The interactionist perspective entreats us to take not society but humankind and its ability to choose and perceive as the primary reality for sociological analysis. Within this view of the actor, the idea of institutions is grasped and understood. However, institutions are not understood as fixed and autonomous, albeit functional, entities. Rather, institutions are to be understood in terms of regularized, conventional, crystallized patterns, or organizations of interaction. To put it another way, we might say that, according to the interactionist perspective, institutions are there, they are real, they do contain and constrain human action but they are there as a result of the history of human interaction, they are embodiments of human choice and perception – they are not 'God-given'. If self is to be seen as a project, then institutions may be regarded as processes. From within this view of the social actor, order is addressed almost exclusively with reference to social relationships. Thus, we would consider how order is achieved through the initiation, maintenance and alteration of face-to-face social encounters.

Symbolic interactionists, in a somewhat non-reflexive manner, often assume that the ordinary member of society operates exactly like the theorist suggests, that there is no sense of transformation from the concrete to the analytic. It is as if their own theory accurately represents or perfectly describes the way people act. We must assume that sociologists and all people live together in a state of 'symbolic interaction' – we might sense a precursor of one of ethnomethodology's claims here.

Adult Socialization

We may now proceed to an investigation of the interactionists' theory of 'socialization' which, along with theories of social control, is always the key to whether a theory is operating with a dynamic view of the social actor. Socialization, for the symbolic interactionists, is a process of the development and subsequent regeneration of the 'self'. Self is an absolutely central concept. Herbert Blumer (1969) has stated that a human being is an organism in possession of a 'self' and what he is meaning here is that the 'self' is a unique property of being human and, indeed, its major distinguishing characteristic. It is the symbolic possession of a self that renders the human being a special kind of actor. The possession of a 'self' transforms the human individual's relation to the world and gives it an original and peculiar character.

In asserting that the individual has a 'self', the symbolic interactionists mean that humankind is able to reflect upon itself, both as a general feature of any situation that it inhabits, but also as a particular identity. Animals, it is supposed, do not have this capacity. The human individual is able to regard himself or herself as both an object and a subject in the world – in the terminology of George Herbert Mead, the human 'Self' is 'reflexive'. The human actor, as a reflexive self, may perceive him/herself, communicate with him/herself, and act towards or in relation to him/herself. In sum, the human actor as a reflexive self is able to become an involved object of his/her own subjective course of action.

Through the capacity of a reflexive self, the individual becomes centred and thus stands, knowingly, in relation to personal sensations and thoughts like wants, pains, fears, goals and aspirations, but also in relation to the non-personal such as the objects in the world which surround him or her. Most significantly, in terms of social life and social action, through the continuous ability to 'reflect', the individual actor learns to perceive him/herself in relation to the presence of other people, their actions and their expected actions. So, apart from forming a strong and centred sense of his or her own identity the individual learns to classify his or her own form of existence and self-presentation as a reflection of the responses that other people make to his or her behaviour. This is a process that the symbolic interactionists refer to as 'identification' or 'self-definition'. It is a process of collectively constructed self-awareness brought about cumulatively through the responses of others in interaction. The process gives rise to what Cooley (1902) has described as the development of a 'looking-glass self', that is, we grow to see ourselves as others see us, we become aware of how we are for others. The mirror metaphor is not, of course, specifically accurate as such reflected images are reversed, however, the point is a good one. We come to know things about our presence in interaction that affect people in predictable ways – but not all!

As a consequence of this continual process of interacting with the self, of perceiving directly in relation to the self, but of also seeing the self as others might see it, the individual is strategically placed to plan, organize and carry out his or her own courses of action. The individual actor can act towards others specifically in relation to his or her own presence. As Blumer has put it: 'Possession of a Self provides the human being with a mechanism of self-interaction with which to meet the world – a mechanism that is used in forming and guiding his conduct.' So the interactionists also seem to be saying that the human capacity to symbolize always instances the other-ness of things or other people. Interactionism, then, is described as a real and practical capacity of human-being, it is alive in the minds and practices of real active people – the social world may be regarded as a unified collection of interacting reflexive selves. The manner in which people escape 'solipsism', that is the belief that the self is all that is the case, is through a sustained concentration on defining the self, not in isolation, but as an object in a world of similar objects. It is as if the individual provides for others, the 'outside', from a strong awareness of self, 'the inside'.

The development of the reflexive self through socialization is seen to be brought about by two complementary processes, the first being the attainment of a language, learning to speak, and the second being the practical experience of interacting with other people. These two processes can be recognized as the 'symbolic' and the 'interactive' – hence 'symbolic interaction'.

The interactionists understand initial or 'primary' socialization taking place through a series of loosely defined stages. It must be emphasized that these stages are theoretically descriptive rather than normatively and chronologically prescriptive in the way that, say, Jean Piaget's steps in human physical and mental development are laid out. At a 'preparatory stage' the human infant is treated as being born non-social. That is, the baby is considered to be an organism, full of potential, but as yet unable to impose sense or meaning upon the world. The infant is initially 'non-reflexive' and rather more docile than it is destined to become. Of course, babies have a presence and a series of wants and needs that are expressed as demands but they are essentially controlled rather than controlling. At the outset, the human infant is not able to join in social interaction but, necessarily, that same infant is not born into a vacuum, he or she is born into a social world, a meaningful world, a communicating world, indeed, an environment that is symbolic.

The interactionists are not entirely explicit about the mechanisms by which a child adopts a symbolic repertoire and thus becomes self in process but their theory of language acquisition seems to follow rather from the ideas of 'behaviourism', that people learn by responding to particular stimuli. What they suggest is that by virtue of being human and alive, the baby will produce a whole range of sounds, gestures and movements and, out of this vast pattern of expressions, certain features are selectively encouraged by the parents. In a sense, meaning is structured upon them, so, for example, ma- and da- sounds are applauded and rewarded and become the initial linguistic categories through which the infant attaches meaning to the differentiation between his or her parents.

Following from the 'initial' socialization, the interactionists talk about the 'play stage'. It is here that the infant imitates the skills and roles of other people in their immediate environment. By various sets of copying procedures the infant practises all the regularized patterns of action that are available within the confines of his or her social world. The various roles that the infant plays are unconnected, they consist of diverse aspects of behaviour learned from particular people or 'specific others'. However, within a child's world it is supposed that some individuals will have greater influence on the child than others and these people are referred to as 'significant others'. For the child the most obvious 'significant others' are the parents, but when interactionists are doing studies of adult socialization a 'significant other' might be the person in an occupational situation who teaches a newcomer the important aspects of their new job. 'Significant others' are, then, the most consistently available and strategically important members of one's immediate social world.

At the following stage, which the interactionists refer to as the 'game stage', the child is seen as becoming more involved, more generally, with other people. By entering into the forms of interaction that are available, the child learns, to some degree, what is expected or required of him or her 'generally' by other people. Beyond simply indulging in private imitation of others that he or she has observed, the child is now placed in a position where he or she needs to come to terms with others, to consider others, and to relate to others in the world. It is at this 'game stage', the stage involving general interaction with others, where the individual finally de-centres, abandons solipsism, ceases to regard him/herself as all that there is in the world. The child is required, by demands from the outside, to alter the view that everything and everybody is part of or an extension of his or her ego.

The child is, oddly enough, learning to become an active participant in social life but through a necessary acknowledgement of and adjustment to the 'passifying' constraints of other people. The dichotomy between activity and passivity now begins to look less like a pair of radical alternatives and more like a contingency, two aspects of a situation in a necessary, and perhaps even tense, relationship. We have an emergent actor who has achieved this status of being able to choose, decide and evaluate situations in order to act upon them, but only through the acceptance of the idea that he or she is merely part of a situation or a world. And that this world is a shared world, it is populated by others, and these others are conscious and just like him/herself. This recognition of 'otherness' is the way that the interactionists import an idea of social structure back into their theory. Essentially, what we have in the interactionists' perspective is a soft concept of structure, an iron hand in a velvet glove. The interactionists rarely talk about structure but say that individual actors organize their behaviour in relation to a 'generalized other', which is an extremely broad concept, meaning, approximately, all other people and their expectations in an interactional context. Another structural concept that the interactionists employ is that of a 'definition of the situation' and if we enter into or take on a 'definition of the situation' it means that as dynamic actors we nevertheless assume a taken-for-granted and consensus view of the way things typically happen in situations like this! We appear to have reformed the active-passive as a contingency again.

Let us now complete our account of the interactionists' view of the development of the 'reflexive' self. Emerging from the 'game stage' the young person now views him/herself as an active partner in situations but also views him/herself in terms similar to those which can be applied to others. The child perceives him/herself as situated, interacting with others, interacting on the same terms with self, the child is, indeed, becoming 'reflexive'.

G.H. Mead – the 'I' and the 'Me'

George Herbert Mead states that the 'reflexive self' is comprised of two elements which he refers to as the 'I' and the 'Me'. They provide a microcosmic instance of the tension between individual and collectively oriented dispositions. The 'I' is that inner, personal, essential element of individuality, it is the immediate, continuous and non-reducible different self-consciousness of the particular person. The 'Me' is the organized and routine set of attitudes of other people that each and every individual takes on board through the process of socialization. The 'Me' is that aspect of self which is cumulatively available in the social arena; it is that aspect of ourselves, or outside presentation of self that is most readily communicated with others in interaction. We are both personal and private and also public and shared, we are both active in our conduct but also docile in our responses. It is interesting to note the parallels between the 'I' and the 'Me' and the 'Ego' and the 'Super-ego' that Sigmund Freud was writing about at the same historical period.

What we have established so far is an outline of the interactionists' theory of socialization and the meta-theoretical model of the actor that stems directly from this. We also have an outline sketch of the city and the seemingly sympathetic concerns of this school of theorists. At its kernel what we have heard is an account of the intense relation between space and control. Think small-scale, think small group, think contextual meanings, and seek to explain the totality as if it were an accumulation of the particularities forged by dynamic individuals engaged in the continuous process of interaction and negotiation. The space is simultaneously social and geographical – 'turf', 'zones', 'districts', all comprising an intricate ecology which is as much society as it is the city. The perfect conditions for the conception of a subcultural theory. Just as the interactionists' theory of socialization was about change, process and renewal, so, in macrocosm, was the Chicagoan's burgeoning theory of the city.

Issues of Urban Culture

Robert Park, who joined the department at the University of Chicago in its early days around the outbreak of the First World War (which did not engage America for three more years) had previously been a successful and committed journalist. He was no hack searching out sensation but rather the natural-born *flâneur* who regarded his city as a complex of stories waiting to be told. As such, his transition from newspapers to urban sociology was simple and seamless. Within a short time of having joined the department, he had established his status and a reputation and produced a manifesto for the Chicago School that would extend for decades of highly successful work. This manifesto was his ground-breaking essay with Burgess, 'The City: Suggestions for the Investigation of Human Behavior in the Urban Environment', which he first published in the *American Journal of Sociology* in March 1916 and has subsequently been much republished. What the paper reveals, and also instils as core elements in the Chicago urban cultural/subcultural tradition, is a number of features, both motivational and conceptual. First, there is an overwhelming enthusiasm for and absorption in Chicago as a site. Of course the ideas and theoretical frameworks were intended to be transferable but the fervour for this particular city, its history, its structure and its demography demonstrate a kind of intense micro-, local 'nationalism'. Though it pre-dates Sinatra we can almost hear his classic jingoistic refrains in the background ('My kind of town, Chicago is'; 'on State Street that great street', etc.); the city and its interrogators never exhausted their relationship – Chicago never seemed to get over-researched. For Park and future generations the city's potential was limitless.

Second, there was a sense of mystery. The many faces of this city expressed themselves as a great unknown. This was no mere analytic trope but perhaps a genuine reflection of the way in which the many and different forms of life, cultures, styles and strata were both segregated and hidden from each other. Such divisions and insulation may have been a consequence of structural exclusions, isolationist mechanisms from within or a dynamic combination of both. Chicago comprised a series of closed doors which the academy set out to open.

Third, there was an implicit but certainly present intent to reform. Whereas in the English tradition reform and philanthropy were established as a proper and articulate element of any social science or social commentary, in the USA with its high personal achievement ethic, its culture of 'making out' and its consequent cast of winners and losers, such liberal patronizing motives hardly dare speak their name. Nevertheless the Chicago theorists for generations sought out and honoured the 'underdog', from hobo to junkie.

The fourth element stemming from Park's manifesto, which relates to our second point about closure, is an entirely conceptual issue that informs the Chicago view of both place and space. American sociology, and this is as true for Parsons and the East Coast theorists (whom we shall discuss in Chapter 4) as it was for Chicago, operated with a very concrete version of space. Unlike the postmodern and cultural geographies of today where space can be the conceptual loci of identity, in these early days space was quite literally the physical location of the actors who then acted in relation to those physical surroundings. Space was seen as a series of plateaux or perhaps set stages upon which action occurred, slum districts might correlate with slum behaviour. Pieces of geography became meaningful variables and, as such, context took on an ontological status – place has being. This gives a new reality to 'manors', 'turfs', 'districts', 'islands in the streets', 'ghettos' and 'slums'. We can now begin to appreciate the appeal of the early Chicago obsession with social ecology and we can also see the injection of a hard facticity into the idea of subculture that has, through time, crystallized into the taken-for-granted vehicle to round up, localize, reduce and explain any selected group of people:

> This tension between human ecology as an approach within urban sociology and as a distinct and basic discipline within the social sciences, runs through the work of the Chicago school. It is basically a tension between defining the perspective in terms of a concrete, physical, visible object of study – the community – and defining it in terms of a theoretically specific problem – the adaptation of human populations to their environment ... throughout his writings, Park nevertheless emphasized the ecological concern with the community as a visible and real entity. This confusion, which lies at the heart of the problems associated with human ecology, is reflected in, and was exacerbated by, the ambiguity inherent in Park's concept of 'community', for this term is employed to refer both to the physical community and the ecological process. In the former case it refers to an empirical object of analysis, in the latter case to a theoretical one. (Saunders, 1986: 53)

Social Ecology

Some early awakenings of this, our, subculture, can be found in the urban cartographies of Park and Burgess (1925) and Thrasher (1927), following in the footsteps of Park or indeed, in Burgess's case, actually working with Park. The idea of social ecology became central for a time but its legacy was that it became foundational work in criminology. Concentric zones, radiating out from Chicago's central business Loop (a geographical zone quite literally enclosed by an oval loop of overhead railway lines) were mapped and then analyzed in terms of the constitution and stability of their populations. Instability or 'transition' made for volatility and the greater likelihood of deviance and drift. The contributory variables were poverty, poor accommodation, short-term occupancy, conflicting ethnicity, lower levels of social control. Little Chicagos within Chicago, yet all both instancing and contributing to the character of the whole – again, an analysis that begins from the particular and moves to the generality. Social problems and social pathologies were both traceable and mappable by zones. Burgess developed a range of associated theories including 'succession theory', which informs us of the evolving and almost rippling process of replacement and renewal that moves through the city on an ecological basis; functions and focus shift so slum Islington becomes the home of the Prime Minister, Shoreditch and Brick Lane develop from slum and criminality into trendy and avant-garde. He also produced the idea of 'centralized decentralization', a hydra-like thesis which suggests that the urban organism develops multiple nuclei as it becomes increasingly complex and, given the geographical/ontological preoccupations of the school, it becomes increasingly difficult to determine where the centre of things actually is!

The ecological model necessarily contained a theory of system equilibrium which, in turn, lends itself to the convenience of subcultural theorizing. The logic runs as follows: ecologies exist in equilibrium, the city (Chicago) is to be regarded as an ecological system, yet, empirical evidence reveals that the city demonstrated localized outbreaks of disequilibrium. Should this be accounted for by explanations in terms of individual psychopathology or should we attempt to retain the macrosociological notion of equilibrium by incorporating a series of culturally pathological micro-climates, namely, subcultures? This all begins to sound remarkably Parsonian! The predominant and causal features of the social structures, that is control and solidarity, have in some neighbourhoods been thrown out of balance. Such eruptions might occur through sudden demographic changes like waves of immigration, a decline in the quality of the housing stock or a change in its use. In short, urbanization, urban change and urban growth. Whatever, all the elements of equilibrium remain, but they are somehow scrambled or disordered. The sociological response to this is counter- or sub-cultural formation as the neighbourhood populations do not feel at one with the mainstream population (what Park referred to as the 'natural areas'), they may not even speak the same language.

Just so, Thrasher interprets gang formation and gang life:

> the gang occupies what is often called the 'Poverty Belt' – a region characterised by deteriorating neighborhoods, shifting populations and the mobility and disorganisation of the slum ... As better residential districts recede before encroachments of business and industry, the gang develops as one manifestation of the economic, moral and cultural frontier which marks the interstice. (1927: 20)

This most accurately described the Loop district, the very heart of Chicago, then in a state of considerable transition. Even though Thrasher felt and expressed an intense level of moral repugnance for the gang members and their nefarious activities, he opted for a close, naturalistic appraisal of the gang experience. He attempted to account for gangland activities from the perspective of the gang member, that is, to realize their meaning, structure and their definition of the situation.

The environment of the gang, the street, then becomes not a minefield and no-go area for the decent citizen but a pleasuredrome of excitement, challenge and creativity for the young slum dweller. Such freedom, such as it was, could be juxtaposed with the alternative agencies of social control like homes, school, work and the police. The space engendered the dysfunctional citizen. Indeed, and this is a constant Chicago refrain, the space is indistinguishable from the citizen. The concept of a subculture is a way of masking and articulating this fusion.

In many senses the ecological vision petered out but the idea of zonality was sustained through the notions of community and subculture. Apart from the proliferation of smaller-scale zonal, subcultural, saturations of delinquency, hobo districts, ethnic quarters, and so on, one major study of note was Zorbaugh's *The Gold Coast and the Slum* which emerged in 1929. Zorbaugh's exotic title derives from the extraordinary juxtaposition of two districts on the near North Side of the city: the Gold Coast which takes in Lake Shore Drive adjacent to the lake, this is and always has been the richest and most high status part of the city, and next to it the area around Clark Street (now gentrified) was then the poorest of slums, previously referred to by Nels Anderson (1923) as 'hobohemia' and variously occupied and re-occupied by waves of Scandinavian, Irish, Italian, Sicilian and Afro-Caribbean immigrant populations. This intense proximity of demographic hyperbole, the extremes of 'haves' and 'have-nots', of 'power' and 'dispossession', and of 'stability' and 'transition' were an urban theorist's dream come true and looked to provide exciting data about inclusion/exclusion, boundary maintenance, drift and contagion. However, little of such analysis emerges. Zorbaugh indicates that the districts are sociological entities rather than just economic entities but goes little further than indicating that the Gold Coasters had little sense of community whereas the slum dwellers had rather more and perhaps even a forced proto-cosmopolitanism, but their transitional character, the instability of their relationships (and often personalities) militated against successful integration. Now what this reservation in my reading of Zorbaugh's major study reveals is a critique beyond the *ad hominem*. This study, in common with much of the work of the Chicago School and, I would suggest, in common with much 'subcultural' thinking and research, lapses into a kind of parochial empiricism and a proud justification for such practice. Subcultural studies, exhaustive ethnographies, may well reveal more about a particular group, community, or a district (or all three as if indistinguishable) than any other mode of research practice and this detailed realism is, in large part, their intent. As such, it details, elaborately details, particularity and difference. Now this kind of detail, like biographies and oral histories, provides a wealth of background data and examples but it is, in essence, a-social or non-sociological. In one sense the Chicago School had no theory of society greater than a theory of Chicago (called 'The City'). Such megalithic and totalizing ideas as 'society' were left to the East Coast theorists, like Parsons, who developed them in spades, often without the flimsiest empirical referent. The tradition of subcultures that stems from Chicago, then, is unashamedly micro in its approach, never looks to the bigger picture and is unfortunately ill-equipped to level a critique of the social structure or the going order much beyond its own parish boundaries.

Again, the more fundamental issue here is to do with the actual status of the object of analysis and it is this confusion that is at the heart of the troubles with the Chicagoan's formulation of 'community' and, I would strongly suggest, with subsequent formulations of a sense of 'community' at the hands of subculture theorists. This is a problem also recognized by Saunders (1986) in his assessment of urban human ecology studies which I shall paraphrase as follows: is the community or subculture a real visual object? (do they exist as such?) or is the community or subculture an analytic construct? (is it employed to serve a purpose in theory?). Saunders then directs us to a much earlier critique of the Chicago School based on the same point, and please note – read 'subculture theorists' for 'ecologists' and 'subculture' for 'community' in this context:

> One of their main difficulties lies in the confusion between abstraction and reality. Some of this confusion might have been avoided if the [Chicago] school had been familiar with the 'ideal type' method of investigation. The concept 'community' is approached in a way that denies its social attributes. In its very definition it is an abstraction of the asocial aspects of human behaviour. Yet the ecologists find themselves compelled in many ways to take account of the social factors which in reality are intrinsically related to and bound up with the asocial community. Had ecologists persisted in dealing with the concept of the 'natural order' as an abstraction, or as an 'ideal type', for the purposes of study these social factors could be treated apart from 'community', as conditioning, concomitant and intrusive phenomena of the 'natural order'. We would then have only the problem of the validity and scientific utility of a particular classification and of a particularistic philosophical ideology underlying the delimitation of the category 'community'. But ecologists do not pursue this course consistently; what is to them an abstraction at one time becomes a reality at another. (Alihan, 1938: 48–9)

And it is worth noting that this near contemporary criticism comes from an East Coast scholar, the Parsonian side, where the sociology is much more informed by the European tradition and much more concerned to theorize the collective consciousness.

The 'Underdog'

The ecological elements of the Chicago perspective certainly decreased through time and with the advent of the 1960s the subcultural emphasis became even more pronounced. If the 1960s spoke to the populace of protest, counter-culture, beat poetry, drop-outs, road culture, the hippie movement, recreational drug-taking and anti-Vietnam War sentiments, then parts of the academy, particularly in the USA, met this with a liberalism and a philosophical tendency to cultural relativism. The young Chicago (or neo-Chicago) scholars were well placed to capitalize on this populist wave and the individualism, situation-specificity and relative meanings provided by symbolic interactionism gave rise to the concepts and analytic constructs. Similarly, the now vibrant idea of a subculture captured the idea of specificity and spatially contained any sense of a 'definition of the situation'. Although belonging to a former generation of Chicago scholars, Everett C. Hughes was the prime mover in setting this new wave of studies in motion. His graduate students were the new, active liberal liberationists, all fired up and with an expectant populist audience. Hughes was also concerned that this largely well-to-do set of white, middle-class (mostly male) students should get out into their roaring city and experience life as others had to, the side of the 'underdog'. So a mass of small- to medium-scale empirical ethnographies were embarked upon that variously revealed, revered or defamed (which other group of sociologists would have made a study of the adult socialization of doctors and entitled it *Boys in White?*). Such was the energy emerging at this period that when poor Julius Roth (a contemporary of Howard Becker) was hospitalized with tuberculosis, Hughes, his supervisor, visited him and simply told him to 'get on with it' – the result, an ethnographic, subcultural study of a TB ward called *Timetables*.

Stemming largely from earlier developments in the fields of the sociology of organizations, the sociology of deviance and the theory of identity formation, a new set of concepts and styles emerged like a 'career', 'labelling', 'social reaction', 'typification', and 'transaction'. They were all grand ironies and inversions. A career could mean becoming a lawyer or becoming a mental patient. Labelling meant that, for example, children did not only fail in schools because of their intellectual ability but also because of the typical construct that the teachers held of them based on a moral cocktail of class background, self-presentation, and behaviour. Teachers' interaction with pupils, and their rewards and punishments were then seen to be based on such selective perceptions rather than in terms of outright performance. Social reaction essentially advised that criminal justice was not objective or the outcome of extensive ethical consideration, rather, it was to do with the degree of moral outrage that an act drew forth from the mainstream majority; middle-class office pilfering or use of the work telephone is not the same category of act as, say, shoplifting or petty theft. Typifications could be as mundane as how a cab driver selects a fare to ensure a good tip, or as serious as how the same policeman might view the same act as delinquency or youthful high spirits, according to what part of town he was in, or perhaps the ethnicity of the perpetrator.

So, with a new vocabulary, the Chicago School was back in action exposing, subculture by subculture, the parts of the city and the lives of the inhabitants who they, and a larger academic audience, would not otherwise meet in the common room. Howard Becker, probably the most famous of this whole clutch, gave us *Outsiders*, wherein we learned how to become a marihuana user, and about the alternative life of a jazz musician. Becker's insights were first-hand, no fly on the wall or participant-as-observer he. Becker showed an intimate knowledge of the lived definition of the situation, he knew and told us about the tight-knit and supportive meaning structure. His work was both shocking to the Establishment and a delight to the students of the 1960s. But he, like many of his colleagues, seemed to forget about the social structure (a problem with subcultural studies). All the world is a choice and there appears to be no power or rather, no analysis of power. So, in many ways, Becker and his generation faced the same set of problems as had Cooley and his group of social pathologists with the earlier social pathology work:

> The basis of 'stability', 'order', or 'solidarity' is not typically analyzed in these books, but a conception of such a basis is implicitly used and sanctioned, for some normative conception of a socially 'healthy' and stable organization is involved in the determination of 'pathological' conditions. 'Pathological' behaviour is not discerned in a *structural* sense (i.e. as incommensurate with an existent structural type) or in a *statistical* sense (i.e. as deviations from central tendencies). This is evident by the regular

assertion that pathological conditions *abound* in the city. If they 'abound' therein, they cannot be 'abnormal' in the statistical sense and are not likely to prevail in the structural sense. It may be proposed that the norms in terms of which 'pathological' conditions are detected are 'humanitarian ideals'. But we must then ask for the social orientation of such ideals. In this literature the operating criteria of the pathological are typically *rural* in orientation and extraction. (Wright Mills, 1943: 97)

Another criticism of this extensive body of subcultural sociology also emanates from the left in the form of Alvin Gouldner. Referring to the neo-Chicagoan deviancy theorist, he writes:

[T]heirs is the school that finds itself at home in the world of hip, drug addict, jazz musician, cab driver, prostitutes, night people, drifters, grifters and skidders: the 'cool' world. Their identifications are with deviant rather than respectable society. For them orientation to the underworld has become the equivalent of the proletarian identifications felt by some intellectuals during the 1930s. For not only do they study it, but in a way they speak on its behalf, affirming the authenticity of its style of life. (Gouldner, 1973: 29–30)

He also attacks their frontiermanship and colonialism, themes I shall address in Chapter 7.

So what we have in the Chicago School is over a century of sociological work that demonstrates an intensity in its fecundity and productivity but also in terms of its concerted integration of theorizing and research practice. More than this, there is a calculated concentration of the analytic gaze; Chicago became a metaphor for social life in general. And finally, there is a moral tone, an espousal of the world-view of the outcast, the needy, the marginal and the excluded; yet this itself becomes clouded. The contamination that derives from the coexistence of the high ground and the wild side leads to a suspicion of vicariousness and prurience (confusions not peculiar to this group of sociologists). The combinations of intensity, concentration and focus can readily transmogrify into a kind of conceptual parochialism and such a mindset is most adequately served through the idea of a 'subculture'.

Let us move now to East Coast America and see how the same concept and its forceful implementation arose from a very different set of auspices.

FOUR The Missing Narrative II
Parsonian Systems Theory

In *The Social System* Parsons has not been able to get down to the work of the social sciences because he is possessed by the idea that the one kind of model of the social order he has constructed is some kind of universal model; because, in fact, he has fetishized his Concepts. What is 'systematic' about this particular grand theory is the way it outruns any specific and empirical problem. It is not used to state more precisely or more adequately any new problem of recognizable significance. It has not been developed out of any need to fly high for a little while in order to see to see something in the social world more clearly, to solve some problem that can be stated in terms of historical reality in which men and institutions have their concrete being. Its problem, its course, and its solutions are grandly theoretical. (Wright Mills, 1959: 58)

Thus concludes Wright Mills's (1959) blistering attack on what he sees as the obscure, unworldly and sterile intricacies of Talcott Parsons's grand systems theory. Essentially, he is saying that Parsons has a monotheistic vision of how societies hold together, that such a vision is homespun, calculatedly arcane, unashamedly elitist and, perhaps most important of all, wasteful of the real lived experience of most people. This is a battle of the Titans where Harvard Man meets Maverick Marxist and the young stand by and applaud the latter's assault on the gentle Republicanism politics that Parsons espouses as the key to the social bond. What Parsons's system depends upon is an allegiance to a normative structure which, in itself, is simply taken for granted. So, as Wright Mills stated earlier in his tirade:

Now, what Parsons and other grand theorists call 'value-orientations' and 'normative structure' has mainly to do with master symbols of legitimation. This is, indeed, a useful and important subject. The relations of such symbols to the structure of institutions are among the most important problems of social science. Such symbols, however, do not form some autonomous realm within a society; their social relevance lies in their use to justify or to oppose the arrangement of power and the positions within this arrangement of the powerful. Their psychological power lies in the fact that they become the basis for adherence to the structure of power or for opposing it. (1959: 46)

So perhaps Parsons had the right problem but viewed it through the wrong coloured spectacles. Clearly, it is this political perspective that informs his theory of subculture yet we need to know far more about his total social system before we can even appreciate why he should have needed to make recourse to subcultures at all given his vast armoury of explanatory devices. Back to the beginning.

The Oversocialized Conception of the Actor

Aaron Cicourel (1964), when writing about the problems that arise in establishing appropriate forms of method and measurement in sociology, states that 'any attempt at theory or any views on method and measurement in sociology presuppose a certain view of the actor' and he demonstrates this through a review and analysis of different methodologies, such as participant observation and content analysis, within sociology. The significant point of his thesis is that the theorist's initial conception of the actor, the actor's motives and orientations necessarily predispose the character and form of the subsequent theorizing. This is no ethnomethodological conspiracy fable, rather it is a reflexive account of how theorists are never innocent, never neutral in respect of value. It also tells us how accounts of the social world bear a formal relation to their authors' preceding political, moral and personal agendas. More strictly put, theories are informed by meta-theories. This is nowhere clearer than when a sociological programme reveals its theory of becoming, learning or socialization. It is then that we need to ask, in what form of status relation do the social actor and the social structure stand?

A classical style of socialization theory, central to this chapter, begins from a specific and given model of the dominant social and cultural formation (which enshrines the theorist's purpose) and relentlessly strives to subvert and restructure the child's or becoming adult's potentially dangerous and disruptive difference into a form that equates with the inexplicable grounds of the initial theorizing. The learning individual's volatility is stabilized, its riotousness quelled. Such theoretic transformation generates what Wrong (1961) has termed 'the oversocialized conception of man in modern sociology':

> 'Socialization' may mean two quite distinct things; when they are confused an oversocialized view of man is the result. On the one hand socialization means the 'transmission of culture', the particular culture of the society an individual enters at birth; on the other hand the term is used to mean the 'process of becoming human' of acquiring uniquely human attributes from interaction with others. All men are socialized in the latter sense, but this does not mean that they have been completely moulded by the particular norms and values of their culture. (ibid.: 190)

Wrong was writing specifically about Parsonian systems theory and structural-functionalism, that he considered to be the dominant and overwhelming theoretical perspective of that period of the 1950s and the 1960s. And Parsons's hegemonic reign over theory persisted despite the broadsides from Wright Mills among others. He describes the predisposition of such thinking as being organized in terms of an 'oversocialized conception of man'. By this he means that Parsons's cybernetic way of supposing that actors' conduct is highly and narrowly determined by the universal and fixed constraints of a social system implies that if such individuals approximate the way that we live in real social life, then far from being free agents, we are, rather, very rigidly coerced, determined and programmed through our socialization, that is, our induction into the rules, the norms and the folkways of modern society. Clearly, Wrong is saying, such 'oversocialized' actors appear to have lost, abandoned or been deprived of the important elements of choice and free will in the world as designed by Parsons. In Parsons's social system, it is generally predicted that the limits of the system are the limits of action. What Parsons is generating here is a passive and what O'Neill (1995) has later referred to as a 'docile' model of the actor brought about through strict and inflexible views on social control and individual socialization. But this is not to argue that those so far cited as holding antagonistic responses to the Parsonian model have grasped the whole picture, or even for the right reasons:

> Parsons necessarily plays down Freud's instinctualism or biologism in order to bring psychoanalysis into the liberal voluntarist paradigm. For this reason he vehemently rejected Wrong's resurrection of the anti-social instincts and his 'undialectical' construct of the 'oversocialized man'. Wrong's argument banalizes the phenomena of social conformity and social conflict and merely undoes a major analytic convergence in the

name of anti-theory. Yet it may well be argued that Parsons's integrative bias overrides Freud's view that ambivalence is the bottom character of our social relations and as such always leaves open the possibility of regression. (O'Neill, 1997: 4)

We will go on to explore the relationship between Parsons and Freud which is central to the constitution of his social system and to his theory of social deviance – the very font of subculture.

Rather than choosing and evaluating a situation, the actor within the Parsonian world always behaves or, we might even say, re-acts under constraint. Because systems theory was certainly a dominant and highly influential canon of sociological reasoning for an extended period, the predominant model of the actor in sociology became a passive one. If we view the body of work within the tradition of sociology, we will find that although the typical models of the actor exist, in reality, along a spectrum, then the two predominant conceptions of the active and the passive have established a formal dichotomy. Any review of the range of theories within our discipline would tend to show that, in general terms, sociologists have opted to focus on either one or the other of these two positions, almost exclusively, for empirical and conceptual reasons. This state of affairs has to some extent given rise to a semblance of an almost sectarian fission in the form of the development of two schools of thought. Active and passive are not equivalent to but do equate with the dichotomy between agency and structure, and in a different context the dichotomy between the philosophies of Idealism and Materialism. Thus, cumulatively, the passive, structurally determined, materially constrained actor has become what Hollis (1977) referred to as the 'plastic man', the malleable or bendable man.

Order and Control

Instancing this very issue, linking models of the actor with theories of action and philosophies of being, Dawe (1970) suggests that in essence there are 'two sociologies'. The two predominant modes of sociology derive from two distinct social doctrines emerging from the Enlightenment. The first of these he refers to as the 'doctrine of order', which gives life to the sociology of systems theory and which is committed to treating social action as being derivative of the system or social structure. The second he refers to as the 'doctrine of control' which provides the basis for the sociology contained within an action frame of reference; in this instance, we have the mode of theorizing which views social systems and social structures (in whatever form) as the emergent products or depositions of social interaction.

Clearly, then, such theoretic transformation as the 'doctrine of order' can be experienced in its finest and most original form in the corpus of Talcott Parsons's *The Social System*:

> The term socialization in its current usage in the literature refers primarily to the process of child development ... However, there is another reason for singling out the socialization of the child. there is reason to believe that, among the learned elements of personality in certain respects the stablest and most enduring are the major value-orientation patterns and there is much evidence that these are 'laid down' in childhood and are not on a large scale subject to drastic alteration during adult life. (Parsons, 1951: 207)

Parsons's work establishes a magnificent structure of social organization integrating the dimensions of action and constraint – a monumental task indeed! This edifice operates at the levels of the economic, the political, the cultural, the interactional and the personal – it is thus intended to both permeate and saturate all expressions of collective human experience. Parsons's Social System constitutes the oneness of the social world through two guiding metaphors, first, that of 'organicism' which speaks of the unspecific, the living and is concerned with content; second, that of a 'system' which makes reference to the explicit, the inanimate and is concerned with form. Through our central concept of socialization, Parsons commits a theoretic violence, particularly upon the learning subject, through seeking to convert their worlds from content to form. It is as if societies are conceived of as living organisms but are everywhere becoming machines. A prophetic and dystopian vision. To reinvoke my original terms, the Social System seeks to transform or merge difference into communality.

Parsons's concerns are grounded in the Hobbesian problem of order, however, within the sociological tradition, Hobbes's Leviathan, the monstrous form of the political state which provides for and simultaneously symbolizes the unity of the people, is supplanted by the concept of 'society'. Society becomes the monitor for all order and it further inculcates a set of rules of conduct which are enforced less by individual will and political sovereignty than by society's own pre-existence. This supra-individual monolith remains the unquestioned origin of all causality and all explanation within an order-based sociological tradition. O'Neill has formulated the problem thus:

> we will uncover the archaeology of docility that runs from Plato's *Republic* through to Parsons's *Social System*. Such an inquiry does not discover a single strategy for the production of the docile citizen. Rather, what appears is a plurality of discursive strategies ... The two registers of docility reflect two sides of the same problem of social control, namely, how is it that individuals can be induced to commit themselves *morally* to a social order that seeks to bind them to itself *physically*, i.e., in virtue of its discovery of certain laws of association. The conventional wisdom holds that Parsons's structural functionalism sublimates the moral question in favour of its analytic resolution, overriding critical consciousness with the normative claims of social consensus. Whether from a Hobbesian or Freudian perspective, sociology has always flirted with the discovery of a social physics ... The dream of the social sciences lies in the search for control strategies that would overlap the micro and macro orders of behaviour in a single order of administration ... In other words, despite the analytic power of the Parsonian vision, the discipline of sociology is not only a cognitive science but a moral science whose object is the social production of a docile citizenry. (O'Neill, 1995: 26–7)

The Social System

To grasp the extent of the constraint that Parsons has solidified and institutionalized into socialization theory, we require a brief rehearsal of the main features of the Social System. Simply stated, the edifice is evolved from the top down. That is, it begins from a presumption of binding central consensus values and trickles down to an anticipated conformity at the level of the individual personality. When Parsons speaks of the production of a general theory of action within the System, he is addressing the persistent translation of universal cultural values into particular social norms and orientations for specific acts. Put another way, he is asking how is it that social actors routinely develop the social norms that inform their day-to-day conduct from the deeply embedded cultural sentiments at the very heart of the Social System. How does the collective consciousness become real in the minds of individual people?

It is the social norms that provide the constraints by which the interaction between the basic dyad of Self and Other is governed (and we should note that 'self' and 'other' are referred to as Ego and Alter in the Parsonian lexicon). Thus, the persistent and necessary translation of cultural values into social norms provides the dynamic within the System. Within the context of Parsons's first metaphor, it is as if the organism pulsates and its life blood circulates from the universalistic centre to the particularistic individual cells that constitute the mass. Social action conceived of in these terms is what Parsons refers to as 'instrumental activism'.

The social norms become axial to the total apparatus; they are realized as both the means and the ends of all action within the System. Beyond this, the social norms also provide the source of 'identity' between the individual actor and the complete System, and the overall social order itself resides in the identity between the actor and the System. The concept of 'identification' is an important one to Parsons and one that he developed from a reworking of Freud. In Freud's theory of psychosexual development the narcissistic infant was thought capable of a primitive form of object-choice, called 'identification', in which it sought an object conceived of in its own image which it therefore desired with an intensity matched only by its love for itself. In Parsons's Social System the social norms are the source of this identity because they reduce the potential distinction between the self and the collectivity by engendering a coinciding set of interests for both the self and the collectivity. It is through this basic identification that individuals become committed to the Social System, that they become claimed as members and, significantly, that their behaviour is coherent. The social norms therefore establish the ground rules of social life and any Social System achieves stability when the norms are effective in governing and maintaining interaction.

We should now look, in broader terms, at how the Social System is constructed and how its multiple segments articulate. At another level this will involve a moral tale of how the living body, the 'organism', is generated but how, through its functioning, it transmogrifies into a machine. In the Parsonian world it is as if life passes into death at the hands of the theorist and that the process of 'socialization' is the key to this mortification.

From the outset the System is confronted by the problem of order, however, it is simultaneously defined by Parsons in terms of that very order. At the analytic level, the social order is maintained by two pervasive system tendencies which are shared by all systems whether they are social, biological, linguistic, mathematical or whatever. These tendencies Parsons calls 'functional prerequisites' and they signify first of all the drive towards self-maintenance and, second, the drive towards boundary maintenance. These functional prerequisites refer to the inside and the outside respectively: the former to the System's capacity to sustain itself, to maintain its own equilibrium and to regulate its internal homeostatic balance; and the latter to the System's continuous capacity to pronounce its difference from other systems, to demarcate its boundaries and thus to stand in a positive and delineated relationship to its environment. We should note that these two systems do emerge primarily from bio-systems theory and they constitute the point at which the metaphors of the systemic and the organic merge and thus the point at which the rule of analysis becomes the rule of nature.

Sub-systems

If we examine the actual framework of the Social System more closely, we find that it is further comprised of three distinct sub-systems. It is the functional interchange between the sub-systems which provides for both the evolution of the overall System and its emergent qualities. This functional interchange between sub-systems appears as yet another sign of life within the machine. The purposes of the sub-systems are to ensure the survival, the maintenance and the growth of the wider System. They are: the 'physical' sub-system, the 'cultural' sub-system and the 'personality' sub-system; and it is the latter which is specifically concerned with the problems of learning, becoming integrated, childhood and socialization.

Routinely, the personality sub-system is presented with the unsocialized child as its focus and its primary reality. The problem that the overall System is addressing here is that of sustaining existing patterns of social interaction in the wider society by invoking and awakening the latent sociality within each child. Consequently this sub-system needs to ensure that the individual is provided with a suitable and conducive environment such that he or she will be enabled to generate the appropriate capacities that are ultimately demanded by the System as a whole. This complex of problems is to be handled practically by the family which acts as the locus of the individual's growth and learning and the affective repository for the total System. The family, therefore, assumes a key role in Parsons's model, it is theoretically operative in successfully conducting the primary socialization but it is also subsequently ascribed the duties of providing the essential emotional support of all of its members -essential, that is, in ensuring their continued functional efficiency. Socialization is clearly no small task. As a concept, it glosses the massive constellation of processes and accompanying para-phernalia that comprise 'person building'. In precise Parsonian terms, socialization involves the lodging of the System's basic instrumental and expressive drives into the structure of individual personalities.

As alluded to earlier, there is a significant psycho-analytic dimension in Parsons's theorizing about the child which appears not simply through his application of certain Freudian categories but more insistently through the urgency with which he emphasizes the need to penetrate inner selves:

> Both psychoanalytical theory and the type of sociological theory which is in process of developing a new type of analysis of social structure and its dynamics go back to the same basic conceptual scheme or frame of reference which it is convenient to call the theory of action. This theory conceives the behaving individual or actor as operating in a situation which is given independently of his goals and wishes, but, within the limits of that situation and using those potentialities which are subject to his control, actively oriented to the attainment of a system of goals and wishes. (Parsons, 1964: 336)

Essentially, the Social System is finally dependent upon the successful capture of total personalities. This capture eclipses the possibility of individual divergence, dissolution, dissent or difference. The System is fed by the compliant personalities of its members and must, perforce, consume difference and divergence.

Parsons and Freud

Despite the compulsive Freudian drive in Parsons's constitution of the child, there is a paradox here, namely, that in a strong sense, personality theory and the consequent specification of childhood emergence are not very important in his work. Parsons parades his primary commitment throughout and this is a commitment to addressing the problems relating to the stability of complex social formations. Personalities are, of course, significant here but their embodiment, namely, social actors, come to be constructed in terms of the features they display that are pertinent to their functioning in the wider context, not those relevant to their difference and individuality. It is their qualities as cogs in the machine that are to be stressed. The System seeks to undermine the autonomy of the Self and any subsequent expression of difference. Following from such an aspiration Parsons's theory is characterized by a stable unitary isomorphism. This entails that all structural aspects of the social world from total social systems, through sub-systems and particular institutions down to the constitution of individual personalities, are to be viewed as formally analogous to one another. Thus, personalities are microcosmically analogous to total social systems; they share the same form, content and repertoire of responses and they are similarly oriented in relation to the same universal set of choices or 'pattern variables'.

With this isomorphism in mind we can proceed to the fundamental elements of the Parsonian personality theory, which he calls 'need dispositions' and which are highly informative concerning socialization theory's conception of the child. The need dispositions display two features: first, a kind of performance or activity; and, second, a kind of sanction or satisfaction. Here then are the perfect ingredients for a homeostatic balance between desire and satiation. At a different level, as it is the case that all 'need dispositions' have built-in regulators, we also witness Parsonian governance at work, namely, the iron hand of coercion concealed within the velvet glove of normative constraint. The essential conceptual model remains that of a naturalistic personality comprised of a battery of 'need dispositions', the gratification of which is neither wholly compatible with nor entirely possible within the personal and material limitations imposed by the social structure. Desire and constraint clash head-on and the outcome is the greater good of the collectivity. It begins to look as if we are witnessing the rebirth of the 'id' which needs to be battened down by the 'super-ego' now emergent in the form of the Social System, and this is precisely the case. The potentially overwhelming 'need dispositions', which are at the same time wholly expressive elements of the individual personality, have of necessity to be integrated, co-ordinated and modified by the value standards and role expectations extant within the System.

As previously found in Freud's theory, in Parsons the social bond is seen to reside in repression. The threat of infantile sexuality and the difference presented by childhood must be treated as pathological. Based on this commitment and given the integrity of a System contingent upon isomorphism, the socialization process (or process of socio-libidinal castration) serves effectively to maintain both the inside and the outside within the requirements of order. That is to say that the socialization process maintains the personality system and by implication the whole social system through the very process of optimizing gratification within the limits placed by the social structure. It is a perfect regulatory mechanism, it both incorporates and contains.

In a strong sense we might suggest that part of the late Parsonian synthesis at work here is the monumental amalgamation of powerful elements of Freud's super-ego with all of the capture of Durkheim's social constraint, and this within a theory of action. The alliance of sociology with psychoanalysis has provided a significant landmark within the human sciences and certainly liberated our potential for explaining human conduct. Parsons, however, unlike Freud before him, was insistent on the integration of the cultural environment with the personality. Without this framework from which to understand the reproduction and acquisition of a generalized level of affective symbols, the workings of the ego become simply cognitive. Thus, feeling and moral constraint remain the province of the super-ego and the 'fierce' theory of socialization persists.

To return us now to our original point, Parsons and the powerful tradition of socialization theory that extends from his work, successfully abandon the becoming individual to the dictates of the Social System. The social practices of growth, development and learning are sublimated by the theorist's presumptive motives in sustaining integration and order at the analytic level. The newcomer, the outsider, the learner, like the deviant, signifies difference. In an unsocialized state the individual actor is manifestly profane, it threatens to bring down social worlds and the threat can only be mollified within theory by treating the child through an archetype as a proto-adult. Thus, socialization theory makes sense of the neophyte as a potential and inevitable supplicant at the altar of the corporate rationality implicit within the Social System. The social practice of child is, therefore, ultimately and necessarily displaced within the discourse of socialization.

Such seemingly bland dehumanization is not uncommon within this form of reasoning. All conventional sociological worlds rest their orderliness upon a strong yet unexplained theory of what everyone knows, that is, upon an ascriptive notion of competence on the part of their members. As a consequence of the adult member being regarded within theory as mature, rational and competent (all as natural dispositions), the learner, the child is viewed, in juxtaposition, as less than fully human, unfinished or incomplete. Such dichotomous discrimination in terms of socio-cognitive competence assumes its most explicit form in theories concerned with the learning process. It is in this context that the idea of becoming adult is taken to delineate a singular and highly specific mode of rationality. Although social theorists are aware that 'rationality' is a collective institution which addresses the relation between self and other, and despite the fact that their studies have shown them that rationality can neither dominate humankind nor be entirely free of its historical context, nevertheless, an irony persists. Within social theory, particular versions of rationality are devised and manipulated in order to contrive the exclusion of certain groups. In learning theory, it is the child who is so excluded.

Socialization, like formal education, like all significant *rites de passage*, is a violent and painful process in the highly political sense that all people are constrained to become some categories of being rather than others. Its weakness, as theory, is to justify its constraint through a naturalistic reduction. Societies and systems of education do not have to be as they are. That they are as they are is the result of a decision, a series of decisions and the routine artfulness of processes of cultural reproduction.

Parsons's Need for Subcultures

Whither subculture? Well, the concept would not have needed to raise its ugly head if the Parsonian behemoth had done its job properly. Or to put it another way, if the oversocialized, passive, docile puppets upon which the Social System depends had through time correctly integrated the appropriate structure of normative value-orientations, then there would be no requirement for either systems or cultures of the 'sub' variety. It is interesting to note in this context the Parsonian application of the prefix 'sub'. While later commentators on the concept are explicit on the point that the use of 'sub'-culture denotes no ranking or moral evaluation, it implies rather an attachment, in inversion or a subordination, but one that is worthy, semi-autonomous, decisive and viable. Parsons is not so sure. Whereas more contemporary theorizing, perhaps more left-wing or even liberal thinking such as that of the Birmingham group or, much later, the Manchester group, might interpret or indeed espouse the political power, the intervention, and the genuine resistance generated by the non-mainstream manifestations of self-supporting social practices and belief systems, Parsons draws a clear line. For Parsons, the 'sub' is the inferior. How can it be else when it works in opposition to the supposed normative order and dedicatedly threatens, through its own mechanisms of reproduction, to challenge or in some way bring down the dominant normative order? For Parsons sub-cultures are bad news but he has had to recognize, as had Durkheim before in relation to crime, that these things exist in society whether we approve of them or not. Parsons manifestly does not approve and the empirical examples of subcultures that he provides are criminal or deviant groups, delinquent gangs and radical ('leftist') political movements – wicked, dysfunctional people all! And in the manner of Durkheim's subtle symbolic use of crime before him Parsons sets out to re-socialize, re-integrate or at least symbolically mainstream the practice of subcultures. A subculture is a collective experience, not an individual act: 'The legitimation of a deviant pattern immediately shifts it from the status of an individual to that of a collective phenomenon. Those whose orientations reciprocally legitimate each other constitute a collectivity which is a sub-system of the social system' (Parsons, 1951: 292). This recognition may provide meta-theoretical 'anchors', 'bridges' and 'patterns of legitimation' that we normative folk are familiar with:

> In general two other sets of factors contribute to the further strengthening of deviant motivations which have an anchor in legitimation within a collectivity. The first of these is the degree of difficulty of stigmatizing the subculture pattern as legitimate in terms of the wider value system. This is a function of what have been called 'bridge' elements between the two value systems ...
>
> The second set of factors which further the claim to legitimation is that involved in the development of a strong defensive morale of the deviant group. (ibid.: 292–3)

The universal salvation implicit in Parsons's recovery of the subcultural member is that in fundamental ways they are very much like the rest of us, they seek recognition, acceptance, thus conformity and an honouring of their motives, even behind the ugly mask of non-conformity:

> the deviant is ... enabled to act out both the conformative and alienative components of his ambivalent motivational structure. To do this he must of course make the substitution of the pattern of the deviant sub-culture for that of the main social system. But having done this, he can be compulsively conformative within the deviant sub-group at the same time that he is compulsively alienated from the main institutional structure. (ibid.: 286)

And like good Durkheimians, subcultural members seek protection from the outside and solidarity on the inside:

> Here the compulsive quality of the need to conform should be kept in mind. This fact may have an important bearing on various features of such delinquent sub-culture groups, such as the extreme concern with loyalty

to the group and the violence if the condemnation of 'ratting'. The need for
ego to feel that he is a member of a group which is genuinely solidarity
and which he can 'count on' is compulsively intensified. (ibid.: 286–7)

They are so very much like us. But wait, we should not be too hasty in
our hierarchical judgements, subculture can allow for the avant garde,
maybe even some discrete sections of the intelligentsia:

The most essential modification of this occurs when adherence to a set of
artistic standards becomes itself the primary symbol of belonging to a
sub-cultural group. This tends to be true of the 'coteries' of the art world,
the schools and the 'little revues'. This is the elevation of what in terms of
general cultural tradition is a secondary basis of institutionalization into a
primary basis for a special sub-culture, one which, by nature of the case
could not become a primary basis of institutionalization of a society. (ibid.:
411–12)

But by and large, subcultures are a rough lot, not 'our sort of people',
and ultimately in contest with all that we value and hold sacred,
despite their spurious claims to a shared system of understanding.
Parsons then turns his attention to

the deviant sub-culture. Here, as illustrated by the case of the delinquent
gang, there is an explicit lack of appeal to legitimation in terms of the values and ideologies of the wider society, there is an open 'state of war'. But
within the deviant collectivity there is very definitely a value-system and
hence an ideology. This ideology will always include a diagnosis of the
basis for the break with the main society and its value system ... there will
be such beliefs as that 'you can't win' in the wider society, that 'they're out
to get you'. (ibid.: 355)

Subcultures as Deviant Behaviour

For Parsons the generation of subcultures is the overflow of a rocky
ride set in motion by an individual's pathological variance from anticipated reciprocity. A critical element of the common cultural patterns
which comprise every set or manifestation of social action, is normative. Patterns are established and there is an expectation that social
members will confirm to those patterns. Approved or 'acceptable'
behaviour within any society is that which implies a complementarity
of expectations – these are the common standards upon which we all
depend in order to give both structure and reliable meaning to our

lives. Deviance embodies a resistance to conformity, its persistence implies that new or different social expectations are thrown up, and their maintenance relies on such resistances and expectations counteracting the mechanisms of social control. Such a process might occur within the environment provided by a subculture:

> Deviance and the mechanisms of social control may be defined in two ways, according to whether the individual actor or the interacting system is taken as the point of reference. In the first context deviance is a motivated tendency for an actor to behave in contravention of one or more institutionalized normative patterns, while the mechanisms of social control are the motivated processes in the behavior of the actor, and of those actors with whom he is in interaction, by which these tendencies to deviance tend in turn to be counteracted. In the second context, that of the interactive system, deviance is the tendency on the part of one or more of the component actors to behave in such a way as to disturb the equilibrium of the interactive process (whether a static or a moving equilibrium). Deviance therefore is defined by its tendency to result either in change in the state of the interactive system, or in re-equilibration by counteracting forces, the latter being the mechanisms of social control. It is presumed here that such an equilibrium always implies integration of action with a system of normative patterns which are more or less institutionalized. (Parsons, 1951: 250)

So there we have it! The disequilibrium wrought through a 'motivated tendency' to contravene should be repaired and equilibrium restored through the exercise of either internal or external mechanisms of social control. However, what a subculture may provide is a haven from the mechanisms of social control and a context within which contravention may become realized as itself normative behaviour. Two difficulties continue to present themselves from within the Parsonian system: the first is the spark or germination of the 'motivated tendency' to contravene; the second is the constitution of the social structure of the subculture. With reference to the first, is Parsons saying that the tendency is endemic but mostly contained (or repressed) or is he saying that only some individuals demonstrate this tendency? Whatever, he seems to be saying that although most aspects of human action emerge from an interaction and integration between the social structure and the personality, when we come to consider deviance (or non-conformity), then our explanations are thrown back upon the personality. With reference to the second, it is hard to see the space or indeed the ease within the constitution of the social system that allows for the generation, let alone reproduction, of 'havens' or enclaves that remain insulated from the constraining powers of the normatively oriented values. Could it be that given particular stressful structural conditions, emergent in the pursuit of systems imperatives, that certain groups or individuals become more disposed to contravene than would normally be the case. So, for example, mass unemployment, poverty, economic depression might motivate theft. However, even if this were Parsons's position, he would still be confronted with the Durkheimian problem of why, in the end and whatever the structural constraints, only some people exercise such motivation and not others (not everyone occupying Durkheim's categories of suicidogenic currents actually opts for self-destruction).

Whether we like it or not, the individual seems to emerge as the source of pathology within this model and, fatefully, this would seem to be the case. When building his social system Parsons, the 'incurable theorist',[1] is not writing a naïve utopian novel nor is he describing a science fiction world of the future. Sheltered as Harvard may have been, Parsons still lived in the real world and shared the realities of violence, criminality, deviance and war. What he was constructing was a grand theory for sociology, a level of theorizing not previously aspired to or reached, even Robert Merton, his contemporary, decided to stop short and opt for 'middle range theory' (1949). Thus, as with Weber (one of Parsons's sources of inspiration) and his ideal-types, the exact relation between the theoretical construct and empirical reality is problematic in every particular case. So Parsons sets out his stall in his Introduction:

> The subject of this volume is the exposition and illustration of a conceptual scheme for the analysis of social systems in terms of the action frame of reference. It is intended as a theoretical work in a strict sense. Its direct concern will be neither with empirical generalization as such nor with methodology, though of course it will contain a considerable amount of both. Naturally the value of the conceptual scheme here put forward is ultimately to be tested in terms of its usefulness in empirical research. But this is not an attempt to set forth a systematic account of our empirical knowledge, as would be necessary in a work of general sociology. The focus is on a theoretical scheme. (Parsons, 1951: 3)

This is not to say that Parsons has no responsibility for the goodness-of-fit of the system to the empirical world but it does show, and quite explicitly, that his priorities were elsewhere. It also enables us to see that a 'subculture' for Parsons is a theoretical trope, a sub-clause, a device to assemble and contain that which escapes the larger picture. This does not mean that he approves, but *The Social System* is only covertly a moral tale. As Gouldner noted:

the central focus of strain in Parsons' social system is 'deviance' – lack of conformity with moral norms – but not lack of gratification ...

Parsons is undoubtedly correct in indicating that variations in the degree of moral conformity with a system have an effect on its stability. Yet this says no more than that moral conformity makes some independent contribution to system stability. It fails, however, to assess the contribution that may be made by sheer gratification, by gratification independent of morality. Parsons tends to reduce gratifications to those derivable from conformity and to emphasize that conformity usually brings gratification. Like Plato, he prefers to believe that the good man is also the happy one. It is easy to understand how a moralist is disposed to claim this, but difficult to understand that anyone describing the world could do so. (1970: 237–8)

Subculture as Transgression

In a peculiar, and perhaps triumphalist, manner the subculture reunites the deviant with the Parsonian collective. The need for a theory of subcultures is a tacit recognition, by the theorist, that the constraints of the social system have not adequately or successfully contained the non-normative differences that individual personalities throw up, from time to time. The tendency to contravene, or transgress, is on occasion exercised so that the motivation of the conduct can no longer be resolved or integrated within the known dominant system of value-orientations. The erratic individual breaks free from the system's gravitational pull and begins to spiral away to oblivion and meaninglessness. Not so, the deviant adheres to other action sets of deviant and non-normative conduct. The deviant recognizes his or her own, but much more than this, the deviant recognizes his or her insuperable need dispositions for adaption, goal attainment, integration and latency – which are to be found in a convenient subculture. The system claims the individual back, the individual expresses their intrinsic social urges and dispositions. Anarchists form societies, and when alcoholics or drug addicts have experienced stigma and exclusion from the mainstream, they achieve recognition and inclusion in the subculture. They cannot be anything but social and subcultures are linked to the mainstream by 'bridges' discussed earlier. They are microcosms and even though their moral core might be disagreeable to the theorist, they are recovered at a higher analytical level. The form of their action is social even if the content of their action is manifestly anti-social. Far from enabling or assisting the expulsion of transgressors, subcultures guarantee their reclamation and incorporation. Parsons's social system certainly pre-dated Foucault's dark surveillance tower, and with a positive spin!

Although Parsons's writing is, at times, difficult and even obscure, his message is never confused. The primary concern is the retention and maintenance of the system at both the highest level of generalization but also at the level of substantive face-to-face interaction. Within such a model both based upon but also evolved through such a cybernetic entelechy, the subculture is no luxury or theoretic delicacy, it is an essential circuit in the management and processing of difference.

We now turn to address some subcultural studies that appear more or less independent of the sociologies that we have looked at so far.

Note

1 Parsons's self-description in the dedication to his wife Helen in *The Social System*.

FIVE Some Anomalous Cases

Although it is always a great convenience to accommodate the world within our classificatory schemes, it does not always fit. Similarly, sociology, like the world, on occasions resists our best attempts to fit it within our categories of schools, perspectives and traditions. In this chapter I have assembled, first of all, a fecund tradition of historical writing from within a distinctly English framework and complex of social conditions. This is the mid-nineteenth-century drive to social reform and its subsequent literature, pamphleteering, social surveys, epidemiology, politics and social policy. Second, I include two sociological studies, of particular note, which although contemporary with elements of my missing narratives of subculture and, in some cases, bearing implicit witness to their presence, appear nevertheless to have emerged independently of their influence or perhaps as an agglomeration of their combined impact. These two studies both emanated from the East Coast of America and were separated by a gap of some thirty years. And, finally, we shall look at a range of classroom interaction studies that occurred within the late 1960s and 1970s' boom in the British sociology of education. These are, in most cases, an unhappy amalgam of both of the 'missing narratives' previously discussed. All of this work either has, or should have, contributed to our contemporary understandings of the meaning and purpose of the concept of subculture in social theory. Integrity demands that I do not shoehorn them into any of the other chapters of the book.

Victorian London

An historical and pre-sociological source of, arguably, subcultural investigation derives from the mid to late nineteenth and early twentieth century and has a substantive rather than a theoretic core. This is the Victorian 'centre' for contemporary cultural studies, the 'centre' being the East End of London and its contributions being Henry Mayhew's *London Labour and the London Poor*, Jack London's *People of the Abyss*, Charles Booth's *Life and Labour of People in London*, Walter Besant's *East London*, James Greenwood's *Low Life Deeps*, the novels of Charles Dickens and Arthur Morrison, and the writings of Henry James, Mearns, Sims, Friedrich Engels and many, many more. These urban spectators picked up on and gave voice to the outcast and inarticulate subjected culture of a working class delineated and ghettoized morally, politically, economically, and even geographically and architecturally. Their work is informed by no clear theory of ideology but by a 'bitter cry' on behalf of 'the whole way of life of a people' informed by observation, demography and epidemiology, and an elementary ethnography. Their practices have been most cynically described in terms that modern 'cultural studies' would equally well need to refute:

> 'being at home in the city' was represented as a privileged gaze, betokening possession and distance, that structured 'a range of disparate texts and heterogeneous practices' which emerge in the nineteenth century city – tourism, exploration/discovery, social investigation, social policy.
>
> A powerful streak of voyeurism marked all of these activities; the 'zeal for reform' was often accompanied 'by a prolonged, fascinated gaze' from the bourgeoisie. (Pollock, quoted in Walkowitz, 1992: 16)

Thus, the *flâneur*, both ancient and modern.

Emerging from this genre of work was a Victorian imperialist cultural tendency to realize the difference between Disraeli's 'Two Nations' in terms of a series of derogatory and evolutionist metaphors. The sensational realism inherent in the factual journalism, fiction, fact(ion), and philanthropic surveys and tracts of the period gave rise to an abundance of colonial 'alterity'. The social world became formulated through conveniently bifurcated signifiers with the normative, respectable, healthy, law-abiding West being offset by the dramatic excesses of 'abysses', 'mean streets', 'outcast Londons', 'low-life deeps', 'jungles', 'thieves dens', 'swamps', 'dark continents', 'wild races', 'wandering tribes' and the almost universally present 'dark' imagery of the working-class areas, and most particularly of the East End of London. The contemporary distillation of these negative loci is the ubiquitous 'underworld' of common currency, the criminal subculture much addressed by sociologists.

Although in most cases the writing of these Victorian philanthropists and reformists was well meant, it was also in part confused in its thinking through an unconscious desire to analytically expel, isolate and categorically expunge the non-normative defilement of less than decent or poor folk. Though sympathetic, the bearers of such sentiments still articulated a near insurmountable gulf between themselves and the group that Marx described as the *Lumpenproletariat*, as we noted earlier in Chapter 2. I believe that such unconscious motivation is a potential feature of all subcultural studies, perhaps most manifest in the Parsonian tradition discussed in Chapter 4.

Gelder has already picked up on this historical invocation of subcultural ideas mostly in quasi-realist accounts of urban low life. He says:

> subordinate and marginal social groups had been accounted for in various ways long before this term [subculture] gained currency. The culture of beggars and vagabonds, for example, was described as far back as the fifteenth century in 'beggar-books' which alerted readers to the kinds of tricks and deceptions these people might practice upon them. By the late sixteenth century, details accounts of the specialized languages of rogues, beggars and cony-catchers (swindlers) were being printed ... By the end of the seventeenth century, and later, an increasing number of specialist dictionaries were being compiled both to register and to explain the otherwise impenetrable argot of particular groups of 'low life' ... We can think of these compilations as early kinds of sociology, often involving extensive contact between authors and informers. (Gelder, in Gelder and Thornton, 1997: 264–5)

The historical gradient to the nineteenth century and beyond reveals for us, albeit from a different set of principles, the contradictions, paradoxes and shortcomings of 'subculture' as a concept in modern sociology. Subcultural thinking in the minds of British Victorian crusaders, pioneers, reformers and moral revivalists reveals the seemingly irreconcilable beliefs of both the liberal humanist and the reactionary, normative conservative. It may be that such antagonisms resided side by side within the mind sets of such thinkers or it may be that such conceptualization enabled an apolitical playground for individuals of oppositional opinions to co-exist. Whatever, the contemporary willingness to formulate the poor and criminal classes into gradations of 'low life' or an 'underworld' could expose the desire to either alleviate or control, or perhaps both. Mayhew forewords his fourth volume of *London Labour and the London Poor*, entitled 'Those That Will Not Work' as follows:

I enter upon this part of my subject with a deep sense of the misery, the vice, the ignorance, and the want that encompasses us on every side – I enter upon it after much grave attention to the subject, observing closely, reflecting patiently, and generalising cautiously upon the phenomena and causes of the vice and crime of this city – I enter upon it after a thoughtful study of the habits and character of the 'outcast' class generally ... Further I am led to believe that I can contribute some new facts concerning the physics and economy of vice and crime generally, that will not only make the solution of the social problem more easy to us, but, setting more plainly before us some of the latent causes, make us look with more pity and less anger on those who want the fortitude to resist their influence; and induce us, or at least the more earnest among us, to apply ourselves steadfastly to the removal or alleviation of those social evils that appear to create so large a proportion of the vice and crime that we seek by punishment to prevent. (1950: 29)

Mayhew says a great deal in this short passage. He sets a diagnosis for contemporary human ills that is social. Then, in the mode of a good sociologist, he moves the etiology of events from the realm of individual will and places it in the context of the social structure. He places in contradistinction the politics of pity and anger, and also the social policies of alleviation and punishment. In a brief, and sensitive, space he invites the reader to investigate his, or her, own value position and also to question his, or her, latent acceptance of the status quo. Yet Mayhew also describes a living reality where folk are designated and life-determined by their place within the division of labour, where the very cultural geography of their identities are fatefully proscribed by their market potential. Intricately interwoven with this picture is the quasi-religious view that work and godliness combine, and that morality *per se* (not merely the prevailing morality) derives from an inner force and a will to self-revival. Fallen women would rise from the *demi-monde*; alcoholics would transcend from the taproom; the thief will discover generosity and the slovenly will celebrate the joys of labour (particularly physical labour). It is no accident that when the mid-nineteenth-century fervour for social reform aligned with the English proto-sociological consciousness (European social theory not yet having crossed the Channel), the mediating form was often the Bible. Charles Booth regaled the underworld from an elevated platform on the strays of Whitechapel and the Salvation Army stormed the hot spots of the low life in his wake. Christian theology takes up and amplifies a Platonic narrative in as much as the power of the light on reality is generated by the Divine Creator and the epistemological quest of the Platonic soul now becomes the metaphysical search for the inner goodness of the Christian soul. Such doctrines privilege the imagination, that which enables us to think outside of ourselves, they privilege the subject and they instil a cultural commitment to overcome or transcend existing social and moral boundaries that restrict our vision and the achievement of the 'good' life.

Subcultural thinking in this early form exposes all of its worst endemic features, yet to confuse decades of sociological theory. It sympathizes, it empathizes, it gives voice, and it politicizes. Yet it simultaneously ghettoizes, patronizes, ostracizes and polices the normative order. Mayhew's table of contents of 'Those Who Will Not Work' is subdivided into three groups: 'Prostitutes in London'; 'Thieves and Swindlers' and 'Beggars and Cheats' – well, that should just about take care of the lower working class! (Just as the designations of Hebdige's youth might be exhausted through the terms 'teddy boys', 'mods' and 'rockers'.)

Which brings us back to Hebdige who, needless to say, acknowledges the significance of the Victorian tradition in the formation of subcultural theory: 'The study of subculture in Britain grew out of a tradition of urban ethnography which can be traced back at least as far as the nineteenth century: to the works of Henry Mayhew and Thomas Archer, and to the novels of Charles Dickens and Arthur Morrison' (Hebdige, 1979: 73). Yet what Hebdige appears to be arguing is that subcultures must have demonstrated some form of ontological visibility in this era, just as they did in post-war Britain, to be taken up in the ways that they variously were. Hebdige's (1983) position shifts somewhat by the early 1980s when he has found Foucault and begins to see the emergence of subcultures at different historical periods as part of different regimes of surveillance. This is a point developed in a sophisticated analytic manner by Tolson (1990), himself a graduate of Birmingham CCCS, as follows:

as Hebdige observes, the conditions within which subcultures first appear as spectacular are themselves related to a variety of strategies for social intervention, in nineteenth century practices of philanthropy, education and moral reform. The important point here is that an early form of cultural research is developed within what Foucault has defined as the modern approach to 'governmentality'. Mayhew himself was at the liberal, reformist end of the spectrum, but he was nonetheless operating within the 'realm of the social', which Paul Hirst has characterised as a distinctively new discursive formation, opening up a range of approaches to the classification, supervision and policing of urban populations. In this light, subcultures can be regarded as one way in which such populations become socially visible and in terms of which they can be categorised. And hence, this early form of (sub)cultural studies, in its concern for the identification and classification of different urban 'ways of life', is bound up with the exercise of new forms of power. (1990: 114)

Tolson further develops his own argument to suggest that within the swathe of Victorian ethnography an analytic and moral process is functioning which apparently resolves the seeming paradox of all subcultural study. That is, the work both realizes the respondents' subjective awareness and meaning structure and yet remains essentially unaffected by it. This simultaneous empathy and exposure Tolson refers to as 'subjectification'.

This argument, though starting from a very different place, is resonant with my own. Subcultures are not things, they are not physical or even social entities, they are ways of seeing. What informs that way of seeing might be, as the Althusserians and later the Foucauldians suggest, the exercise of new forms of power. What might also inform that way of seeing from within a sociological tradition is a rejection of holism, an abandonment of grand narratives, a shift from the macro to the micro, a slippage of belief in the efficacy and causal impact of the social, a concession to the cult of the individual, overall, a break with modernity's project. Over a century of subcultural studies have done little to resolve the difficulties and paradoxes first revealed in the middle-class perambulations 'in Stepney, Whitechapel, Poplar, St. George's-in-the-East, Limehouse, Bow, Stratford, Shadwell, and all that great and marvellous unknown country which we call East London' (Besant, 1882: 3). Nor has such work sought to empower the weak, the poor and the downtrodden any more than Hebdige's supposition that 'style' constituted political resistance, however deeply unconscious that may have been.

Another commentator on Mayhew, from outside of a sociological tradition, has remarked:

Mayhew's work on the costermongers enabled him to grope towards the concept of sub-culture which he could not, in the end, successfully formulate. For some time he had become more aware of varying cultural patterns and ... gave noticeably more space to corporate social characteristics ... But the costermongers presented a group whose lives were based on a code of shared meanings as different from that of other London workmen as from respectable middle class Englishmen. Yet the system of values seemed coherent and consistent in itself. When he returned to the costermongers for the second time ... he produced a full-blown cultural study, treating them at length as a group with distinctive social habits. He discussed the conditions of the trade, their amusements, politics, sex habits, religious attitudes, education, language and dress.

He tried to inform and generalize his discovery of a sub-culture by developing current ethnological notions into the category of wandering tribes in civilized society. (Yeo, in Thompson and Yeo, 1971: 86)

'Successfully' is the key word here, perhaps the concept of a subculture resists successful formulation in anyone's hands.

East Coast Mavericks

One primary study of subculture which has been a methodological landmark for generations of sociologists and which one has to respect for withstanding the ravages of time is William Foote Whyte's study of *Street Corner Society* (1955). Whyte was an economist by training, graduating from Swarthmore College in 1936 and moving to Harvard on a three-year Fellowship. Now Parsons was on the faculty at that time but as a junior member, not much more advanced in his career than Whyte. He published *The Structure of Social Action* the following year but *The Social System*, the true formulation of his views on subculture, did not appear until 1951. Parsons's influence in the mid-1930s was not such that it would have impacted on Whyte's thinking and there is no evidence that they ever met. No lineage here despite the geographical alignment. Certainly, the Chicago School had been formed since the turn of the century and was moving into its middle generation of Hughes, Blumer and Warner. There has been a suggestion that Whyte was in part influenced by the latter, yet as Madge (1963) points out: 'He [Whyte] found that in 1936 he could obtain little help from the existing literature. Lloyd Warner's *Yankee City* series had not yet begun to appear, although his work in Newburyport had started' (Madge, 1963: 213), and Madge continues:

There were only two books that seemed relevant. One was Carolyn Ware's *Greenwich Village* and the other was Lynd's *Middletown*. He was somewhat disappointed in both of these because they seemed to be rooted in social problems, whereas Whyte was more concerned in the first instance to study the social system. He wanted to see how a local community worked rather than to study its particular social difficulties. He had been reading Durkheim and Pareto. (ibid.: 213)

So no apparent Chicago contamination either, except that in the Preface to the enlarged edition the author offers thanks to Everett C. Hughes and Buford Junker (both of the University of Chicago) 'for reading the Appendix [addressing research procedures and methodological issues] and for their useful comments', so this is after the event of the actual research taking place. Whyte appears to have discovered subcultures for himself with the unlikely assistance of Elton Mayo, the father of the human relations school of organization theory – he awakened Whyte to social psychology and face-to-face methodologies.

Whyte's work is rather disarming in two ways, first, that he is amazingly open and straightforward about himself, his background values and his research intentions and second, that he has all of the appearances of a 'natural' sociologist in manner, in ethnographic style and in his ability to communicate the way of life of a people. Although his sociological sophistication and research skills grow demonstrably as the study evolves, it is clearly his innate 'people skills' that enable his progress. He sets out predisposed to a model of the social system that is a mosaic, a pattern of subcultures set in juxtaposition with the dominant moral and normative order, which are marked out by social exclusion from the outside and self-sustaining insulation from the inside. There he was in Boston, always a smart town but always with a shadow side (even today with its drugs and HIV population), and Whyte sets out to find himself a 'slum'. Now a slum is a concept not dissimilar to an underworld in that it takes more for granted than it critically addresses. We might suggest that a 'slum' is an objective description of an urban area marked out by poor housing stock, but it is also, and actually, a moral judgement about the lifestyles of the people and families and social classes and ethnicities and nationalities that occupy such housing stock.

> In the heart of 'Eastern City' there is a slum district known as Cornerville, which is inhabited almost exclusively by Italian immigrants and their children. To the rest of the city it is a mysterious, dangerous and depressing area. Cornerville is only a few minutes walk from fashionable High Street, but the High Street inhabitant who takes that walk passes from the familiar to the unknown.
>
> For years Cornerville has been known as a problem area, and, while we were at war with Italy, outsiders became increasingly concerned with that problem. They feared that the Italian slum dweller might be more devoted to fascism and Italy than to democracy and the United States. They have long felt that Cornerville was at odds with the rest of the community. They think of it as the home of racketeers and corrupt politicians, of poverty and crime, of subversive beliefs and activities. (Whyte, 1955: xv)

Whyte later settles on a slightly less contentious definition of a slum when he ascribes it to 'overcrowding', clearly a structural problem, one constituted through external pressure and not lapsed into through a weak or irresponsible version of agency.

Despite Whyte's easy manner, he experiences the luck that good research projects sometimes do, he found access, or rather he had it found for him. Methodological textbooks speak of the importance of 'gatekeepers' who can be courtiers to a royal household, head teachers to schools or gang leaders to urban 'slums'. In practical terms, the gate-keeper is the individual who provides *entrée*, who shows the researcher the ropes, who affects the introductions, who accesses the argot – who legitimates the interloper! At another, more analytic level, it is the gate-keeper who, premised on the segregation and sovereignty of subcul-tures, opens up or indeed builds the bridges that Parsons was so fond of referring to as re-integrative devices. The gatekeeper is the transla-tor who enables the transmutation of the researcher. It may be prag-matic, it may be conventional, but the employment of such a device implies an initial disbelief in communication, a human fracture, the knowledge of asociality. In effect, such relationships are usually driven by a sense of urgency that forbids the usual pace of socialization. For Whyte, the gatekeeper was the all-powerful Doc, a kind of small-scale, local godfather. Unusually combining a fierce reputation with an extensive knowledge, a sharp intellect, a high level of articulacy and relative youth (he would be nearly one hundred today!). Through Doc, Whyte lands on his feet, he is inducted into the Nortons, Doc's gang. This, combined with his rooming with the Martinis, a homely matriar-chal family who ran a local restaurant, enables him to become launched. Nevertheless, as Whyte will later reflect, he will never quite become accepted a one of the boys:

> At first I concentrated upon fitting into Cornerville, but a little later I had to face the question of how far I was to immerse myself in the life of the dis-trict. I bumped into that problem one evening as I was walking down the street with the Nortons. Trying to enter into the spirit of the small talk, I cut loose with a string of obscenities and profanity. The walk came to a momentary halt as they all stopped and looked at me in surprise. Doc shook his head and said: 'Bill, you're not supposed to talk like that, it doesn't sound like you.'
>
> I tried to explain that I was only using terms that were common on the street corner. Doc insisted, however, that I was different and they wanted me to be that way. (Whyte, 1955: 304)

Clearly their difference from Whyte in terms of social class, education, background and mode of speech were less disintegrative for them than for him. His downmarket patronage was unrequired and perhaps their less normative, more modern sense of a pluralist society could more readily accept and understand difference and divergence without the framing of transitory collectivities within the concept 'subculture'.

From his opening largesse 'Do you want to see the high life or the low life?' (and Whyte saw both), Doc's own position changes. From sponsor and guide Doc becomes friend and collaborator, and Whyte is reflexive about this. In a strong sense *Street Corner Society* becomes Doc's story in Whyte's words, which is not to detract from Whyte's achievement. Whyte becomes identified as 'Doc's man' in the eyes of the Nortons which has implications for his access to data and Doc becomes identified with Bill Whyte, which has implications for him long after the researcher has returned to Harvard.

Following three decades after Whyte, and certainly paying homage to *Street Corner Society*, we find the work of Elliot Liebow. In 1967 he published *Tally's Corner*, a powerful and moving study of great insight. This ethnography bears the subtitle 'a study of Negro streetcorner men', an assembly of signifiers that must already have been slipping into political incorrectness during that early post-Kennedy era, chosen perhaps to shock and ironize the Washington consciousness.

In many senses, if Whyte theorized the stabilities and solidarities of 'slum' communities, Liebow completes the project by revealing their instabilities, fragmentations and volatilities thirty years on. The world had changed and even the subcultures were conceptualized to think in opposition to holisms and total societies are recognized to be barely clinging on to sociality in a rapidly transforming social structure. Liebow certainly positions himself in relation to Whyte's work; he also footnotes and references Chicago scholars from Burgess, Albert Cohen and Everett C. Hughes, through Cloward and Ohlin to Howard Becker. With the exception of Whyte, however, these citations are very much in the background. They demonstrate thorough research rather than direction, guidance or inspiration. In short, they do not constitute a tradition, Liebow is no Chicagoan.

Tally's Corner was written originally as Liebow's PhD thesis in anthropology at the Catholic University of America. Subsequent to its publication as an academic monograph, its author went into public health research and I have no knowledge of him producing any further work specifically within the canon of the social sciences. Even the PhD was not conceived as a piece of blue-sky research, Liebow was already working as a contract researcher on a study of child-rearing practices among the poor under the auspices of the Washington Health and Welfare Council, and the project's director encouraged him to include the 'streetcorner men' as a subject for engagement. The work is redolent with its desire for policy engagement, it is also incredibly humanistic, sensitive and even poetic in its recognition of ironies of social research as a basis for a relationship:

> the wall between us remained, or better, the chainlink fence, since despite the barriers we were able to look at each other, walk alongside each other, talk and occasionally touch fingers. When two people stand up close to the fence on either side, without touching it, they can look through the interstices and forget that they are looking through a fence. (Liebow, 1967: 251)

With the further realization that: 'I used to play with the idea that maybe I wasn't as much of an outsider as I thought. Other events, and later reading of the field materials, have disabused me of this particular touch of vanity' (ibid.: 249); and the conclusion: 'In retrospect, it seems as if the degree to which one becomes a participant is as much a matter of perceiving oneself as a participant as it is of being accepted as a participant by others' (ibid.: 256).

Liebow's framework for analysis, though he never once employs the concept of subculture to describe his own work, derives from what he perceives to be an inaccessible and thus unresearched segment of the population. He begins with the pressing issue of poverty, he aligns it to the structural issue of ethnic stratification, though he does not invoke the process of discrimination that we now readily name as racism. Poverty studies of black families mostly engage with women and children, so he intends to seek out and explain the missing segment of the demography, the absent, poor, black male. He sets out from an implicit description of structural discrimination and the spirals of deprivation that stem from it, he then goes in pursuit of the missing variable. Will this mission, if successfully completed, provide us with an overall integrated picture of the social? Liebow alludes to comparative statements and generalizable data but then strikes us with his manifesto on behalf of the particular:

> The present attempt, then, is not aimed directly at developing generalizations about lower-class life from one particular segment of the lower class at a particular time and place but rather to examine this one segment in miniature to attempt to make sense of what was seen and heard, and to offer this explanation to others. (ibid.: 16)

101

Surely a compounding of social exclusion with an analytic exclusion. Hanging out with Tally, Sea Cat, Richard, Leroy and the other young black stars might help us to see 'what makes them tick' but will it help us see what makes them 'makes them tick' in the way that they do? Does society here recede into the form of a series of oppositional codes such as 'employment', 'fidelity', 'honesty' and 'reliability' – all echoes of the Parsonian latent normative structure?

The British Sociology of Education

In 1959 Parsons published a paper in the *Harvard Educational Review* entitled 'The school class as a social system' and in 1961 co-authored a paper with Winston White called 'The link between character and society' which in combination were to have a considerable influence in bringing subcultural theory into the British sociology of education which, at that time, was the hot-bed of the development of social theory. Essentially Parsons was arguing that the school and its various social matrices were the focus of socialization. It was at this stage in the life-cycle that most significant development took place, specifically in relation to social reproduction and social mobility. Although social systems in themselves and thus analogous to total societies with overall normative structures and regularized systems of stratification, schools, by dint of their particular function and the relative plasticity of their members exercised original forms of emergent agency. Children could play some part in the determination of their destiny and life-chances. This we might describe as the origin of 'peer group' or 'reference group' studies, clearly another precursor of the notion of subculture. As Banks has stated in masterly summary of this epoch of sociological work: 'Implicit in the concept of the reference group is the idea that the individual will employ the perceived, or possibly imagined, behaviour of his group of reference as a criterion for his own behaviour' (1968: 194), and, indeed, the idea of a peer group (and particularly a negative peer group) gained great currency as an explanatory device in attempting to normalize explosive adolescent behaviour during the 1960s.

The alleviation of the adolescent moral panic was not Parsons's primary intention in the work, rather, he is explicitly concerned with: 'an analysis of the elementary and secondary school class as a social system, and the relation of its structure to its primary functions in the society as an agency of socialization and allocation' (1959: 297).

This is not a foregone conclusion for Parsons, despite the relative stasis and clone-like cultural reproduction that the very idea of a social system tends to imply. Rather, there is a degree of choice and selectivity (namely, social action rather than social structural functioning) that emerges through the election of patterns of normative orientation by adolescents. All of this choice takes place, of course, within a social structural location that is not of the actor's choosing. So we hear that the mediating forum is the peer group, later to become a pupil subculture:

> Peer-group membership is a resultant of the preference of the individual within the available range on the one hand, acceptance by the other members on the other. Broadly then we suggest that the individual headed for higher occupational status will choose peer groups that tend on the whole to facilitate his progress in this direction. But his success in this respect is not only his own doing. He may find it easy or hard to gain acceptance. Though of course there are many complex problems in this area, we suggest that, statistically viewed, the rejections by peer groups of otherwise 'qualified' persons are not likely to be too grossly dysfunctional; and, on the other side, the retention, by peer groups oriented to lower eventual status, of persons of relatively high ability may, again statistically, be related to motivational weaknesses that eventually, in spite of current indications of ability, would impede success when tougher tests were applied.
>
> The broad bifurcation of the peer-group structure ... thus seems to us to be analogous to the two-party system in politics. (Parsons and White, 1961: 127–8)

As ever, Parsons's ideas are largely unencumbered by empirical data and a number of studies seemed to fall into line to supply this need. Notably in the UK the ideas were taken up by an emergent group of upwardly mobile young scholars, many destined to go on to greater things, but all intent on demonstrating the post-war democratization that was occurring through education. Paradoxically, much of their work, in terms of methodologies combining ethnography and participant observation, and its micro-sociological approach, would have been seen as rather more influenced by interactionism than by Parsons. However, what I have described as the two 'missing narratives' in subcultural theory combine with a modicum of balance in this work.

Perhaps the most notable study is that by Hargreaves in 1967, *Social Relations in a Secondary School*. In this work, the author studies staff and fourth year pupils at one Secondary Modern school in the north of England. Initially, Hargreaves was a teacher in the school but after a year could not handle the demands of both roles, so he concentrated on the research, yet the participation was much as a practitioner. He observed, used socio-metric tests, collected teacher ratings of boys' behaviour, checked school records, employed questionnaires and discussion groups. He finds broadly in favour of Parsons's bifurcated peer group structure and he both describes and regards the peer groups as oppositional subcultures.

The pupils in Hargreaves' study were distributed according to a class streaming system, organized and justified in relation to the boys' examination record and prospects. The streams were ranked A, B, C and D in descending order of 'ability' and, as we could now anticipate, the streaming had a notable structuring effect on the social relations between the boys, on the content of their values, on their relation to the general culture of the school and, reciprocally, on the way that the school culture manifests itself in relation to them. Analysis of the patterns of friendship, status hierarchies and forms of behaviour demonstrated for Hargreaves two pupil subcultures; these he refers to as the 'academic' subculture and the 'delinquesent' subculture. As cultural rather than demographic forms, they do not fit neatly into the allocated class streams but, again predictably, the large body of the academic subculture resides in the A stream and the vast majority of the delinquesent subculture are to be found in the D stream, and there is a gradient of membership across the B and C streams.

Hargreaves employs the concept of 'oppositional culture' to shape his data; this is an idea previously used by both Parsons and Robert Merton to indicate, with a judgemental inflection, behaviour that was both concerted and 'non-normative'. So we find the pupil subcultures are competitive to the point of antagonism. The members of the 'academic' subculture are 'swats', they are driven by an individualistic work ethic which they collectively reinforce, they seek to achieve, they defer gratification and they conform. The content of their activities identifies with the teachers' goals and aspirations and the form of their self-presentation appears quiescent and highly regulated. So practically, they are industrious, they do what is asked of them both intellectually and in a disciplinary sense, they do not plagiarize each other's work, they dress appropriately (i.e. 'uniform'-ly) and they are generally well kempt. Each of these manifestations signals an implicit target for resistance and oppositional behaviour by the membership of the 'delinquesent' subculture. Here boys gain prestige and status through fighting and smoking and through the audacity of their 'messing about' both in and out of class. Particular signifiers of 'oppositionality' are to be found in clothing and demeanour; the very notion of uniform calls forth an imperative to desecration. Inevitably, and painfully, these two behavioural manifestations and their variants elicit two sets of teacher typifications and expectations. The world divides morally and intellectually in ways that reflect the bifurcated citizenry in Marx's capitalism, alienated by head and hand. This seemingly non-reflexive phenomenological complex generates the alternative spirals of failure and success that ensure the educational 'self-fulfilling prophecy' (a favourite reductive determinism of the day). Brake, commenting on this genre of work with the benefit of a decade's hindsight, puts forward this useful summary:

> Possible roles within the subculture, 'careers' on which to base the roles, and the meaning of the subculture are essential elements in constructing an identity. For example, the official school role of pupil may be rejected by an adolescent who has a semi-conscious recognition of a structural problem, the failure of school to meet the adolescent's needs due to contradictions in the actual purpose of education. This is experienced as school being perceived as meaningless. The deviant subculture appears as a positive reference group (just as the pupil subculture appears as a negative reference group), which offers symbolic and social support, with the counter-ideological stance to that of school. An achieved alternative identity can be constructed from subcultural elements which is an alternative to the ascribed school pupil role. (Brake, 1980: 40)

Another major study of this era which appeared to espouse the oppositional subcultural model of pupil social relations is Lacey's (1970) *Hightown Grammar*. Lacey also wholly assumes the Parsonian thesis and yet adopts all of the strategies of the symbolic interactionist perspective. He investigates micro-sociological mechanisms to reach for the processes of differentiation and subcultural formation in schools. He reveals mechanisms of differentiation and polarization, both through teacher interaction but, more significantly, within the student body. An unstable but recognizable structure appears within classes and all members have predictable expectations of others' behaviour and performance. Subcultural (essentially anti-cultural) formations ensure further stability and uniformity of response. As Burgess has put it:

> In his study of Hightown Grammar, Lacey identified the social processes associated with streaming which he developed into a model of differentiation and polarization among pupils. Here, he uses the term differentiation to refer to the ways in which teachers categorize pupils on the basis of

their behaviour and academic ability. Meanwhile Lacey argues that polar-ization among pupils is a subcultural formation where pupils oppose the normative culture of the school and form an 'anti-group' culture. he found that those pupils who conformed to teacher expectations and demands and who valued academic success were rewarded, while those who did not were perceived in negative terms.

For the teachers in Lacey's Hightown Grammar ... these processes were related to the streams to which pupils were allocated. (1986: 169)

In a contemporary study Sugarman (1967) reinforced the notion of an oppositional subcultural divide running through secondary school pop-ulations. His questionnaire findings revealed a high correlation between non-normative, non-teacher-oriented behaviour, smoking, drinking, dating and fashion victimization and poor levels of achieve-ment and academic success. As previously, the rates were influenced by the pupils' social class.

Having assembled and corralled our anomalous cases of subcultural studies, we now proceed to an investigation of the most recent and most concerted body of such work. This takes us, in origin, to the UK in the 1970 and more specifically to the Centre for Contemporary Cultural Studies located at the University of Birmingham. As stated elsewhere, it is from this tradition that many people derive their sense of and need to implement the concept of subculture.

SIX The Modern Concept Birmingham CCCS

This book is not primarily about 'cultural studies' but about the concept of subculture. However, although subculture has a long and unconsolidated past within the social sciences it became, for some time, a significant leitmotif within the discourse of cultural studies, most noticeably within the variant which emerged from the Birmingham Centre for Contemporary Cultural Studies (CCCS). So, to reiterate, this work is not simply another contribution to cultural studies but has a wider horizon in addressing the history and application of a conceptual device within the study of culture. Now the two are not incompatible, but the study of culture, which subsumes the cultural studies, derives from a variety of philosophical antecedents and traditions of social theorizing. 'Cultural studies' though drawing variously, and either explicitly or implicitly, from these traditions, is a relative newcomer and claims a difference for itself. I shall attempt here a brief sketch of this difference, or rather identity, and its background. Through this route we will find our way to Birmingham and the distinctive contribution which that school of thought has made to our knowledge and use of the concept 'subculture'.

In no more than the past forty years, initially in Britain and then spreading to North America and Australia, a new realm of research and publication activities has entered the academy under the umbrella of 'cultural studies'. Within that period it has gained a legitimacy and a popularity, both inside and outside the academy, which is indicative of its appeal to important contemporary social currents. Research centres have been established and have flourished, academic appointments have been made specifically 'in' that field (and one notes this in relation to, say, the significance of Durkheim gaining the first European Chair in sociology), graduate and, more recently, undergraduate degree programmes have been set up, numerous journals have been launched and heavily sub-scribed, and publishers have designated lists and promoted editors wholly in terms of 'cultural studies'.

So what is it? It is in many senses a hybrid and an ill-disciplined hybrid. Nevertheless it has developed and expanded in the United Kingdom both during the Harold Wilson Labour government boom in university provision and the support of critical thinking but also through the Margaret Thatcher and Keith Joseph period of Tory monetarism when the social sciences more generally were under threat. To have gained support for and enabled such expansion, cultural studies must surely have had a strong and influential parentage or practised the artful political complexion of a chameleon. Neither of these assessments is strictly true. On the issue of lineage, Stuart Hall (1981) has produced the clearest account of a family tree which other, more recent, biographies have assumed as fact and reproduced. Yet this rush of biographies (see also Turner, 1990, and Agger, 1992) itself, all prior to even a fiftieth birth-day, and a constant 'origins' introspection on the part of even its leading practitioners (see, for example, Johnson, 1983) reveal a bastard child des-perately insecure and in search of a parent figure. And on the issue of political complexion one might suggest that the hue was predominantly pink – if not recognizably Marxist, then certainly socialist, or at least social-democratic – with a commitment to unfashionable values like con-flict and radicalism, reform and democratization. Yet neither of my two previous assessments is strictly false either.

Theorizing of Cultural Studies

Hall's hagiography for 'cultural studies' points, rightly, to beginnings not so much in terms of continuities as in terms of fractures:

> In serious, critical intellectual work, there are no 'absolute beginnings' and few unbroken continuities ... What we find, instead, is an untidy but char-acteristic unevenness of development. What is important are the significant *breaks* – where old lines of thought are disrupted, older constellations dis-placed, and elements, old and new, are regrouped around a different set of premises and themes ...
>
> Cultural Studies, as a distinctive problematic, emerges from one such moment, in the mid-1950's. (Hall, 1981: 19)

He elects a solid triumvirate of men-and-their-texts as formative and epoch-making. The three masters are Richard Hoggart and his *Uses of*

Literacy (1985), Raymond Williams with *Culture and Society* (1963) and E. P. Thompson with *The Making of the English Working Class* (1968). Hall is modest in under-stating his equivalence to these figures. However, we are introduced to an impressive gathering and one notable also for its disciplinary location within the humanities and literary studies, rather than the social sciences. Perhaps part of their very acceptability was the capacity to popularize social scientific issues from within 'respectable' disciplines. All three of the cited progenitors, to varying degrees, were equally at home within the lecture theatre, the Arts Council, BBC 2's *Late Night Line Up*, the political rally and university administration. All three managed to theorize the social and political grounds of culture without the militant taint of the social sciences, at that time identified with long hair, leather jackets and campus marches and sit-ins.

Hoggart, for example, in his Preface, lays out a sociological problematic with a literary 'distancing':

> I am inclined to think that books on popular culture often lose some of their force by not making sufficiently clear who is meant by 'the people', by inadequately relating their examinations of particular aspects of 'the people's' life to the wider life they live, and to attitudes they bring to their entertainments. I have therefore tried to give such a setting, and so far as I could, to describe characteristic working-class relationships and attitudes. Where it is presenting background, this book is based to a large extent on personal experience, and does not purport to have the scientifically-tested character of a sociological survey. There is an obvious danger of generalization from limited experience. I have therefore included, chiefly in notes, some of the findings of sociologists where they seemed necessary, either as support or as qualification of the text. I have also one or two instances in which others, with experiences similar to mine, think differently. (Hoggart, 1985: 9)

Nevertheless, Hoggart, Williams and Thompson are collected, by Hall, as the 'caesura' from which 'cultural studies' sprang because all three treated working-class culture (with a disregard for the 'culture debate' over cultural stratification into high, low or mass) as active, coherent, intelligible, located within history, and – even though all three worked within Marxist materialist traditions – not solely reducible to a developing set of economic conditions. This important sense of 'agency' in culture is well established by Thompson when he tells us that:

> [the growth of the working class] is revealed, first, in the growth of class consciousness: the consciousness of an identity of interests as between all these diverse groups of working people and as against the interests of

other classes. And, second, in the growth of corresponding forms of political and industrial organization. By 1832 there were strongly-based and self-conscious working-class institutions – trade unions, friendly societies, educational and religious movements, political organisations, periodicals – working-class intellectual traditions, working-class community-pattern, and a working-class structure of feeling. (1968: 27)

They did not arise as a simple and inevitable epiphenomenon of the factory system.

It is, of course, possible to over-emphasize the communality of vision between these three figures. Hoggart's recollections of Hunslett are deeply impressionistic and carry, within their care and anger, a romanticism bordering on sentimentality. The upshot of this is a model of culture which, although vibrant and valuable in its own right, is nevertheless passive, receptive and tending towards complacency. Williams has a much more voluntaristic view of culture and sees it as a dynamic. But despite his illumination of working-class culture as real and not merely the overshadowed residue in a high culture-dominated society, his Leavis-like view of culture as a totality incorporates the former and enables it to contribute, thus deradicalizing its potential. Thompson, Marxist from the outset, forbids the notion of a common culture and predicates his account on autonomy, challenge, conflict and, above all, class struggle.

Culturalism and Structuralism

Hall, beyond introducing Hoggart, Williams and Thompson as forebears of 'cultural studies', further divides its contemporary practice between 'two paradigms' – the *culturalist* and the *structuralist*, the difference being that in *culturalism* 'the stress is placed on the *making* of culture rather than on its determined conditions'; and in *structuralism*: 'the stress is placed on the specific nature of those supposedly irreducible formal properties which characterize the structure of different types of signifying practice and distinguish them one from another' (Hall, 1981: 10–11).

The triumvirate are all *culturalists* and the *structuralists*, though an imprecise category, are broadly followers of de Saussure, like Lévi-Strauss, Foucault and Barthes. Hall's two paradigms live on, though less contentiously than before, with the British historicists resisting the generalizing and decontextualizing theoreticity of the structuralists with their all-too-comprehensive and deterministic conception of ideology. However, the development of a neo-Gramscian perspective through the work of the Birmingham Centre for Contemporary Cultural Studies, under the directorship of Hall himself, meant that a softer mediation between agency and all-encompassing structure was provided through the concept of *hegemony*. Because of this cultural studies was saved from an early, and wasteful, internecine conflict.

> I have said enough to indicate that, in my view, the line in Cultural Studies which has attempted to *think forwards* from the best elements in the structuralist and culturalist enterprise, by way of some of the concepts elaborated in Gramsci's work, comes closest to meeting the requirements of the field of study ... They constantly return us to the terrain marked out by those strongly coupled but not mutually exclusive concepts culture/ideology. They pose, together, the problems consequent on trying to think *both* the specificity of different practices and the forms of the articulated unity they constitute. They make a constant, if flawed, return to the base/superstructure metaphor ... on the solution of this problem will turn the capacity for Cultural Studies to supersede the endless oscillations between idealism and reductionism. They confront ... the dialectic between conditions and consciousness ... they pose the question of the relation between the logic of thinking and the 'logic' of the historical process. They continue to hold out the promise of a properly materialist theory of culture. (Hall, 1981: 36)

This was Hall's manifesto for the Centre. And it was certainly the establishment of the Birmingham Centre for Contemporary Cultural Studies (CCCS) in 1964, originally under the direction of Richard Hoggart but subsequently, and most notably, under Stuart Hall himself for over a decade, that did more than any other intellectual or institutional initiative in this country to provide a solid and recognizable foundation for what is now known as 'cultural studies'. The Centre generated a shared problematic around a Gramscian sense of ideology, a set of, albeit loose, methods and strategies for research (such as ethnography), and a particular range or perhaps strata of substantive topics primarily lodged in 'subcultures'. Beyond this, the Centre gestated a group of young, ambitious and multi-disciplinary theorists within an imaginative postgraduate programme who graduated out into sociology, psychology, education, film, media, cultural and communication studies departments and providing a momentum of enthusiasm, research and publication that has not waned up to the present (many of them now comprise the professoriate). In this way the CCCS itself has constituted the 'third paradigm' of 'cultural studies', and its network. However, although the activities of the postgraduates and research officers working at Birmingham around this time are often, no routinely, assembled as a cohesive and integrated block of activity some commentators have looked positively at the roots of their disjunctions:

> That designation – 'Birmingham School' ... homogenises and abstracts a body of work from its real conditions of production: the real conditions were heterogeneous and interactive with research outside. Hence, a number of caveats must be entered into the account.
>
> First, participants in the Birmingham School of the 1970s did not always see eye to eye with one another on all aspects of youth cultural analysis: the comparative exclusion of girls from the earliest research is the best known case in point. Second, their subsequent work, as we shall see, diversified to a certain extent. Third, the Birmingham research on youth culture and consumption from the heyday of the 1970s is significant for its synthesis of disparate theoretical traditions, underpinned by a certain populist sentiment, owing much to various strands of American sociology of deviance, including the anomie paradigm, labelling theory and naturalistic methodology, which had already informed the National Deviancy Symposium from the late 1960s. Fourth, the Birmingham Centre's reputation for innovative youth cultural study, however, is well justified because of its distinctive combination of sociological deviancy theory with neo-Gramscian hegemony theory and Barthesian semiology. Working-class subcultures of 'resistance' ... were read *politically* as symbolic challenges to the dominant culture, not as signs of social pathology. It is this committedly oppositional account of subcultural creativity 'from below' that I consider to be populist and which some other commentators have called 'romantic'. (McGuigan, 1992: 89–90)

I have quoted this passage at length because it both honours and deflates the claims made by and on behalf of this body of subcultural study, it also shows its connection to the 'missing narratives' that I have previously discussed. It also resonates with my attempt throughout to refer to the Birmingham group, rather than School.

We might note in passing that, despite the manifest success and external appeal of the CCCS, its scholars and its research output over a quarter of a century, the University of Birmingham eventually incorporated it in the Department of Sociology and then, in 2002, closed it down as part of an economic restructuring exercise.

Gramsci and the Concept of Hegemony

What, then, are we to make of Birmingham CCCS's intellectual development of the work of Antonio Gramsci, the Italian communist, whose writings have been seen to 'broaden, "democratize", and enrich Lenin's strategy of socialist revolution' (Boggs, 1976: 12)?

Because of his political beliefs Gramsci was incarcerated in the inhuman conditions of Mussolini's prisons, a subjection which claimed almost a quarter of his short life. Through his original address of role of the intellectual, the necessity of an active cultural politic, and the analysis of hegemony, with its necessary resistance through counter-hegemony, Gramsci provided for a different kind of understanding of and engagement with popular culture:

> The more the cultural life of an individual is broad and well-grounded, the closer his opinions are to the truth, they can be accepted by everyone: the more numerous the individuals of broad and well-grounded culture, the more popular opinions approach to truth – that is to say contain the truth in an immature and imperfect form which can be developed till it reaches maturity and perfection. It follows from this that the truth must never be presented in a dogmatic and absolute form, as if it were mature and perfect. The truth, because it can spread, must be adapted to the historical and cultural conditions of the social group in which we want it to spread. (Gramsci, 1971: 261)

These ideas, combined with elements and revisions from Althusser, have become very influential in the development of cultural studies and the sociology of culture in Britain. The scope of Gramsci's substantive interests is attested to by the magnitude of topics that are addressed in his major work, *The Prison Notebooks*, ranging from education, philosophy, issues of gender, history, the intelligentsia, and specifically culture itself. The single identifying feature is, however, the generation and elaboration of an original Marxist theory suitable for the analysis of the conditions of an advanced capitalist culture.

Gramsci's thought reveals an active and volatile theorist who emphasizes the intentional character of political action in opposition to those theories extolling the inexorable and deterministic laws of capitalist development. The path to socialism is neither singular nor straight, and requires a relocation of the individual in the vortex of revolutionary struggle. To this end, his own writing was always conceived of as a revolutionary act, not an act of speculation or description, but a dynamic in the process of change. This drive is to be systematically fired by the cultural critic's internalization of the notion of 'praxis'. The conscious unification of theory and practice, logos and eros, thought and action, subject and object. Life is project and project is polemic:

> The philosophy of praxis is a reform and a development of Hegelianism; it
> is a philosophy that has been liberated (or is attempting to liberate itself)
> from any unilateral or fanatical ideological elements; it is consciousness full
> of contradictions, in which the philosopher himself, understood both indi-
> vidually and as an entire group, not only grasps the contradictions, but
> posits himself as an element of the contradiction and elevates this element
> to a principle of knowledge and therefore of action. (Gramsci, 1973: 404–5)

The most significant contribution of Gramsci's thinking to the Marxist
tradition, and also to the analysis of social and cultural formations, has
been through his original discussion of the nature and functioning of
ideology through his concept of *hegemony*. This concept, most particularly, updates the theory of ideology into the context of late modernity.
Whereas Hegel had divided authority into the two spheres of 'political
society' and 'civil society', Gramsci reworked this distinction into the
operation of two modes of control, being domination and consent. The
former is the hard and brutal edge of power, more typical of an older
order in society. Modern political structures function through the allegiance and incorporation of the controlled. The implication here is of a
politic of voluntarism; the ideological strategy is, in fact, one of coercion, persuasion, and cooperation but the coercion is 'soft', the persuasion 'hidden' and the cooperation 'one-sided'; what remains is the
appearance and experience of voluntarism. Hegemony is the principle
that enables this tacit consent through popular 'consensus'. Hegemony
mediates between the individual and the exercise of choice, and hegemony permeates the structures within which choices are made possible; it alters our knowledge about the world. 'The realization of an
apparatus of hegemony, in so far as it creates a new ideological soil and
determines a reform of consciousness and of the methods of knowledge, is a fact of knowledge, a philosophical fact' (ibid.: 365–6).

All elements of the superstructure contrive to exert ideological hegemony within the culture, such as religion, to education, the mass
media, law, mass culture, sport and leisure, and so on. Within an
advanced mass society with mass education, mass literacy and mass
media all operating through a high level of technology, the centre of
power becomes far more adept and artful in reaching out to embrace
the periphery:

> The 'normal' exercise of hegemony in the area which has become classi-
> cal, that of the parliamentary regime, is characterized by the combination
> of force and consensus which vary in their balance with each other, with-
> out force exceeding consensus too much. Thus it tries to achieve that

force should appear to be supported by the agreement of the majority, expressed by the so-called organs of public opinion – newspapers and associations ... Midway between consensus and force stands corruption or fraud (which is characteristic of certain situations in which the exercise of the function of hegemony is difficult, making the use of force too dangerous). (Gramsci, 1975: 638)

Outside of the institutional context, hegemonic power is rendered viable and permanent through cultural values, norms, beliefs, myths and traditions which appear to belong to the people and have a life outside of particular governments and class systems; they nevertheless serve to perpetuate the going order. Modern politics administrate not so much through power as through authority, and authority require acquiescence or 'legitimacy'. Because such a system invites, and depends upon consent, it rewards its populace with cultural stability; a fact of their own making.

> The fact of hegemony undoubtedly presupposes that the interests and tendencies of the groups over which hegemony is to be exercised are taken into account, that there is a certain equilibrium of compromise, that, that is, the ruling group makes sacrifices of an economic-corporate kind, but it is also indubitable that such sacrifices and such compromises cannot effect what is essential. (Gramsci, 1973: 161)

Gramsci's analysis of the role of intellectuals in the cultural process (an issue always critical to Marxist theory as intellectuals are either in the vanguard of reaction to social change or are the essential class traitors in the march to revolution), is to both democratize the role and then to incorporate its specialisms and vitality. The democratization takes place by dispossessing the group of the ownership and production of culture, to be intellectual is a universal function:

> Each man, finally, outside of his professional activity, carries on some form of intellectual activity, that is, he is a 'philosopher', an artist, a man of taste, he participates in a particular conception of the world, has a conscious line of moral conduct, and therefore contributes to sustain a conception of the world or to modify it, that is, to bring into being new modes of thought. (ibid.: 9)

The sphere of intellectual activity within a society, therefore, does not belong to a cultural elite who practise a specialized cognitive style and a shared epistemology, but rather it manifests itself as an integral segment of political action that is rooted in the daily lives and culture of the people as a whole:

> The mode of being of the new intellectual can no longer consist in elo-
> quence, which is an exterior and momentary mover of feelings and pas-
> sions, but in active participation in practical life, as constructor, organizer,
> 'permanent persuader', and not just simple orator. (ibid.: 10)

Gramsci then describes the two kinds of intellectual, the 'traditional' who upholds the old order (and bears a striking resemblance to the Catholic Church), and the 'organic' who emerges as representative of his time to articulate the new order. They are, respectively, part of the problem and part of the solution.

Althusser's Concepts of Ideology and Interpellation

Such ideas resonated with certain of Louis Althusser's (1971) concepts that were emerging in the 1960s. Althusser, having assimilated and adapted some of Gramsci's ideas about 'hegemony' and the distinction between political and civil society, was attempting to theorize about the subtle mechanisms of control, at work in advanced capitalist societies, that enabled the maintenance of a particular social order, a particular set of relations of production and a particular exercise of power without that power being felt. Althusser believed, quite rightly, that modern power is no longer forceful, omnipotent and excessive but rather that it is exercised by stealth. Instead of individuals being regimented and directed, or even manipulated, they are incorporated. Through his notions of the 'repressive' and the 'ideological state apparatuses', Althusser informs us of both the 'iron hand' and the 'velvet glove'. Concretely, he is talking about the police and the armed forces as opposed to education, mass media and belief systems, analytically, he is revealing that the modern state fails in its desire to rule by consent if the populace comes too much into contact with the hard edge of power. The state is seeking the agreement with rather than the coercion of its polity. He develops the mediating concept of 'interpellation', this is the manner in which modern ideologies claim the individual. The dominant ideology operates not as an opaque and compelling wall of ideas that impact upon the consciousness of the collective, rather, they select and individualize and penetrate the subject, thus they invite us singularly into their complex, and once involved, we act as if freely choosing the typical motives provided. The advertisement which 'advises' that to own a particular make of car is to display your obvious sexual prowess is not intended for your neighbour; the headteacher's cry of 'that boy!' across the packed assembly hall renders every pupil vulnerable to the status, and responsibility, of potential miscreant; and the billboard that exclaims 'Your Country Needs You' is certainly not speaking to the person standing behind you. Althusser's ideas concerning interpellation contributed to the burgeoning body of work on cultural reproduction by indicating the routine and systematic ways in which stasis is achieved within culture with the quasi-conscious compliance of the individual member of that culture.

How, then, does this matrix of neo-Marxist theorizing relate to the emergent study of subcultures, so central to the activities and reputation of the CCCS? In a now classic positioning paper first published in 1976 (but cited here through the 1981 edition), four of the leading figures – John Clarke, Stuart Hall, Tony Jefferson and Brian Roberts – make the link that would prove paradigmatic. They adhere to the view that culture constitutes the way of life of a people and, further, that cultures comprise 'maps of meaning' that are both cognitive structures but also tangible structurings of social relations that cohere. Within any one society there are levels at which culture is shared and intelligible to all members but culture is also stratified in line with the differentiations marked out primarily by social class position. Therefore, cultural experience and the organization of social relationships are various but are also proscribed by access to power in society. The power-based differentiation is critical. The general, shared, common culture (all ideological terms) can be realized as the 'dominant culture' and its transmission is handled by various state apparatuses which serve to reproduce its dominance. It is dominant, then, in as much as it is hegemonic, as we have previously discussed. Now subcultures may be modifications, differences, oppositions or resistances but they all exist in a relation to the dominant culture. Thus:

In modern societies, the most fundamental groups are the social classes, and the major cultural configurations will be, in a fundamental though often mediated way, 'class culture'. Relative to these cultural-class configurations, *sub*-cultures are sub-sets – smaller, more localised and differentiated structures, within one or other of the larger cultural networks. We must, first, see sub-cultures in terms of their relation to the wider class-cultural networks of which they form a distinctive part. When we examine this relationship between a sub-culture and the 'culture' of which it is a part, we call the latter a 'parent' culture ... Sub-cultures, then, must first be related to the 'parent cultures' of which they are a sub-set. But, sub-cultures must *also* be analyzed in terms of their relation to the dominant culture – the overall disposition of cultural power in the society as a whole. Thus we may distinguish respectable, 'rough', delinquent and the criminal sub-cultures *within* working-class culture: but we may also say that, though they differ amongst themselves, they *all* derive in the first instance from a 'working-class parent culture': hence, they are all subordinate sub-cultures, in relation to the dominant middle-class or bourgeois culture. (Clarke et al., 1981: 55–6)

So the relation of the subculture to other forms is critical because it directs us to the issue of power, its appropriation, exercise and reproduction. As Hebdige said:

The term hegemony refers to a situation in which a provisional alliance of certain social groups can exert 'total social authority' over other subordinate groups, not simply by coercion or by the direct imposition of ruling ideas, but by 'winning and shaping consent so that the power of the dominant classes appears both legitimate and natural'. Hegemony can only be maintained so long as the dominant classes 'succeed in framing all competing definitions within their range', so that subordinate groups are, if not controlled; then at least contained within an ideological space which does not seem at all 'ideological': which appears instead to be permanent and 'natural', to lie outside history, to be beyond particular interests. (1979: 15–16)

Resistance Through Ritual

Clarke et al. continue to argue that subcultures coalesce in relation to content, that is, their structure and form are determined by the primary and distinctive practices of a group. The degree of distinctiveness ensures the degree of insulation and boundary maintenance from the parent culture. In turn the degree of distinctiveness provides for the possibility of opposition or resistance to the parent culture. This is a point made forcibly also within the canon of the CCCS through the slogan (and title) *Resistance Through Ritual* (Hall and Jefferson, 1975). Subcultures are, then, subordinate, in that they are oppositional, and they are political, in that they are oppositional. They are also both conscious and unconscious in relation to their access to and exercise of power. As such, they may be unaware of their potential challenge to the going order but also and equally unaware of their part in supporting and reproducing the going order by upholding the dominant normative structure precisely through that resistance. This sounds like Parsons in reverse. The CCCS scholars further refine their chosen object of concern by showing a preference for tightly delineated subcultures with strong identities and instance the major post-war generational issue of non-compliant youth as demonstrating an archetypical self-replicating mechanism for the formation of subcultures. Thus, 'youth subcultures' are born, conceptually, as an important (though entirely self-selected) modern phenomenon. So the cult of the white male adolescent as a focus for a considerable body of work became established and with a political justification.

> To locate youth sub-culture in this kind of analysis, we must first situate youth in the dialectic between 'hegemonic' dominant culture and the subordinate working-class culture, of which youth is a fraction. These terms – hegemonic/corporate, dominant/subordinate – are crucial for the analysis, but need further elaboration before the sub-cultural dimension can be introduced. Gramsci used the term 'hegemony' to refer to the moment when a ruling class is able, not only to *coerce* a subordinate class to conform to its interests, but to exert a 'hegemony' or 'total social authority' over subordinate classes. This involves the exercise of a special kind of power – the power to frame alternatives and contain opportunities, *to win and shape consent*, so that the granting of legitimacy to the dominant classes appears not only 'spontaneous' but natural and normal ... The terrain on which this hegemony is won or lost is the terrain of superstructures; the institutions of civil society and the state – what Althusser and Poulantzas, somewhat misleadingly, call 'ideological state apparatuses'. (Clarke et al., 1981: 59)

The optimism inherent in this tradition of theorizing and research is rife. The subcultures to which they attend, the 'working-class' subcultures, are viewed as islands within the political economy. They are sites or spaces wrested from the constraints of capitalism and the dominant order. Even though conceptual, these spaces are spoken of through mostly geographical metaphors such as 'turf', 'territory', 'terrain' and 'space' and the boundaries, which enable entry or exclusion, are marked out by language and style. As Hebdige puts it, 'The meaning of subculture is, then, always in dispute, and style is the area in which the opposing definitions clash with most dramatic force' (1979: 3). A strong sense arises that the subcultures of the working class are not ideological, rather, they are both victories and they are oppositional. This is a forceful claim. The style of working-class youth subcultures signifies a politic which is reflexive and counter-hegemonic. The clothes, the language, the self-presentation and manner cannot be viewed in conventional terms, indeed, Hebdige critiques the commentators who find a compelling aesthetic in such style. These manifestations have to 'mean and mean again', they work outside of the conventional view of the world; they resist assimilation. Instead of 'revolting into style', they 'style into revolt'. This all implies strategy and intentionality and agency. But will this do? Does over-consumption signify protest? Does the biker's leather jacket, the jeans, the kaftan, the tab collar, the dreadlocks evolving into Lacoste and Ralph Lauren logos really announce to the parent and parental culture 'get out of the new road if you can't lend a hand'? Is this the mechanism of the historical process and if 'the times are a'changing', then might not these supposed political assemblies (in the form of subcultures) simply divert an impotent political will from a recognition of the real contradictions at work? Even Hebdige is drawn to a pessimistic conclusion concerning both the penetration and veracity of the political agenda at work in Birmingham-style subcultural studies:

> we should be foolish to think that by tackling a subject so manifestly popular as youth style, we have resolved any of the contradictions which underlie contemporary cultural studies ... It is highly unlikely, for instance, that the members of any of the subcultures described in this book would recognize themselves reflected here. They are still less likely to welcome any efforts on our part to understand them.

And terminates with:

> The study of subcultural style which seemed at the outset to draw us back towards the real world, to reunite us with 'the people', ends by merely confirming the distance between the reader and the 'text', between everyday life and the 'mythologist' whom it surrounds, fascinates and finally excludes ... it would seem that we are still, like Barthes, 'condemned for some time yet to speak *excessively* about reality'. (Hebdige, 1979: 139–40)

Style and *Bricolage*

Perhaps the key to self-conscious realisation of resistance through style lay in what Hebdige and others called *bricolage*. This concept, borrowed from Lévi-Strauss, via Clifford Geertz, designates the practices of a primitive cosmologist (*qua* mythologist) in placing an order upon the chaos of reality without the assumption of scientific or even dominant classificatory categories. This combination of 'primitiveness', which we could take to imply fundamental or inherent artfulness, and the ability to think outside of the box is the sign of youthful *praxis*. This is the source of their active, conscious minority resistance as opposed to the simple, and market-driven anticipation, that they would passively consume fashion. Well, this may be about an awakening and a waning of political consciousness but it might also be about shifting patterns of consumption linked to shifting patterns of the overall standard of living. Muggleton, writing two decades on, and with an eye to revealing subcultural formations and significance among 'postmodern' youth, speculates on the very concepts derived from Marx and neo-Marxisms by the Birmingham group being themselves potentially elements of an Enlightenment modernity. In this sense, such concepts do not readily apply to the ironies and paradoxes of the postmodern condition and the subsequent re-styling of style:

> So does the postmodern trend towards stylistic eclecticism, ironic over-loading and the destruction of historical referents finally result in the 'death of the social', a total loss of meaning? Perhaps, like their attitude towards God, Baudrillard's masses retain only the image of fashion, 'never the idea'. Similarly Jameson's 'breakdown in the signifying chain', which leads to a destruction of narrative utterance and its replacement by the intensification of aesthetic 'affect', can be interpreted as having identical consequences for fashion. In both cases, meaning gives way to spectacle. Style is now worn for its look, not for any underlying message; or rather, the look is now the message. (Muggleton, 1998: 176)

White, Male, Working-Class Youth

In many ways the whole rich, and seductively readable, canon of the Birmingham group's work can be seen as a series of exercises in narrowing or focus. All of this work, both analytical and empirical, was carried out with considerable zeal and with a buttress of justification that, on occasion, seems to rationalize the manifest pleasure that the authors derived from their chosen subject matter. Whereas both Parsons and the Chicago School, in their very different ways, had employed the concept of subculture to investigate non-normative, non-mainstream, deviant, marginalized, minority, class, racial, criminal, unemployed, 'underdog' groups within their social milieu, for the Birmingham people 'youth', and mostly white, male, working-class youth set their parameters. The reasoning behind such exclusivity ran as follows: post-war English society was experiencing a condition of rapid and destabilizing change and this change was impacting significantly on the class structure and on the systems that maintain power and control. The perceived most sensitive index of this instability was working-class youth and its relation to what Clarke et al. (1981)

described as its parent culture. If future analyses sought to link image and reality, that is, ideological form and actual form through the highly visual, 'spectacular' (in the sense of Guy Debord's 'society as spectacle'), then a newer and more historically appropriate understanding of the contemporary exercise of power would emerge. The utter visuality of these youth groups was taken to be highly significant, they had emerged as both perceptual phenomenon each with their own 'look' or 'style', and they had emerged as a political phenomena in that they now impacted on the order of the day. Both Hall and Hebdige have referred to youth subcultures as 'noise' (a concept which communications theorists employ to mean anything that gets in the way of ordered communication). This apparently new and embodied noise was to be seen as it stood in relation to working-class culture (its 'parent' culture), the dominant culture (the normative structure wherein power legitimates stratification), and the mass culture (the context of popular culture, mass-produced, market-driven, ideologically juxtaposed to high culture). Post-war youth demonstrated many non-solidaristic elements with the class culture of its parents and, indeed, the post-war aspirations of its parents were often complicit in this desire for change and an unwillingness to accept the status quo. So youth became a vehicle for anti-establishment currents; or so it was seen. Youth may simply have been and always will be a diversion. The consciousness, and self-consciousness, of youth were adopted by both cultural analysts (and the mass media) as a vector of instability in relation to systems of stratification but also the social structure as a whole. Any shift in patterns of consumption, lifestyle, leisure and self-presentation by youth might signal a collapse of the old order. Thus, attention to a particular form of dress was not a sign of uniformity and containment but rather a sign of positive engagement with the going order. This must have been music to the ears of the entrepreneurs who were running Carnaby Street and the Kings Road and valuable news for the moguls running the recording companies of the era. This 'youth' was no rebel without a cause, there was no nausea or alienation, perhaps it took the failure of Revolution 1968 or the deaths on Kent Campus, Ohio, to instil these sentiments. Or perhaps this 'youth' was, as previously suggested, the optimistic articulation of a different, higher level and somewhat removed political agenda of one wing of the intelligentsia.

Nevertheless 'youth' and 'youth subculture' became an area of expertise, we were invited to follow Barthes and Eco in a semiotic reading of the signs and the more 'hip' or 'with it' the analyst, the greater the vocabulary of signs that came into play. 'I know these kids ...' became the opening salvo in media (and academic) punditry. Here was a new form of inverted elitism, but the strain caused by this narrowness or focusing were beginning to show:

> Very little seems to have been written about the role of girls in youth cultural groupings ...
>
> Female participation in youth cultures can best be understood by moving away from the 'classic' subcultural terrain marked out as oppositional and creative by numerous sociologists. Girls negotiate a different personal spaces from those inhabited by boys. These in turn offer them different possibilities for 'resistance', if indeed that is the right word to use. (McRobbie and Garber, 1975: 25, 36)

Another major figure to emerge from the Birmingham group was Paul Willis who contributed several significant subcultural studies for our attention but perhaps none made a greater impact than his *Learning to Labour* (1977). This is a fine ethnographic study, well researched and well presented with an astounding and original message which countered much of the established orthodoxy in the British sociology of education. It also reveals some of the fundamental paradoxes at the heart of subcultural study. The book opens with the much quoted and quite shocking statement:

> The difficult thing to explain about how middle class kids get middle class jobs is why others let them. The difficult thing to explain about how working class kids get working class jobs is why they let themselves.
>
> It is much too facile simply to say that they have no choice. The way in which manual labour is applied to production can range in different societies from the coercion of machine guns, bullets and trucks to the mass ideological conviction of the voluntary industrial army. Our own liberal democracy is somewhere in between. There is no obvious physical coercion and a degree of self-direction. This is despite the inferior rewards for undesirable social definition, and increasing intrinsic meaninglessness of manual work: in a word its location at the bottom of class society. (Willis, 1977: 1)

The tone and vocabulary of this quote are both challenging and revealing. Although the work is about, in an inverted sense, an anti-determinacy, its supposed elevation of agency in the historical process is, in itself, highly deterministic. We need to unravel this further. The new, subtle versions of ideology at work here, deriving from Gramsci and Althusser, as we have already discussed, no longer view social and cultural reproduction as the outcome of the brute force of

capitalist social structures in collision with the disempowered ideas
of self-determination at work in working-class consciousness. What
we have here is no crude and blanket conception of alienation but a
creative and innovative process whereby working-class youth con-
spire in the development of anti-achievement mechanisms and
rewards that positively accelerate selection and stratification. So the
Hammertown boys, presumably in common with working-class boys
up and down the country, are wilfully complicit in their failure to
achieve academically and therefore achieve upward mobility or better life chances. Failure then becomes, ironically, a sign of counter-
cultural success and a feature of personal identity, and, as such, class
identity works through personal and social identity. Integrity is
retained at all levels and the divisive system maintains an equilibrium with all, manifestly, satisfied by that state of affairs. Such a system would seem to mark the end of false consciousness and kiss
goodbye to the revolutionary consciousness.

What has happened here is that the 'subculture', of working-class
male youth is treated as a microcosmic system isomorphically analogous to the total working-class consciousness. Surely a move in a
Parsonian game, not quite what is expected from a critical theorist. The
weakness is that the analytic capture that is contained within the concept of subculture is blurred with an empirical capture. The penetra-
tions and oppositions that subcultural manifestations were meant to
epitomize are here transformed into implements of acquiescence and,
at a different level, the cultural elements that any 'subculture' may be
supposed to display become continuous with social structural elements
and political elements. Willis's sleight of hand was to appear to replace
choice in the vocabulary of working-class agency and then expunge it
through the collective ethic of the working-class subculture. Both
Hargreaves (1967) and Lacey (1970) a decade before had noticed that
not all people, 'youths', can be simply assembled according to a class
subcultural category, some became 'teacher-oriented' – Parsons (1959)
had noted that. Perhaps one answer lies in not asking the question that
seeks self-confirmation or not anticipating the self-confirmatory
answer. So, if you want to know why young people take up smoking,
ask the ones who do not smoke why they resisted the peer-group (subcultural) pressure.

Of course, Willis was not as blinkered as this suggests, but the use of
subcultural frameworks does insist on both closure and internal uniformity. At a late stage of the analysis Willis introduces the following ideas
to mediate the totalizing effects of what has gone before:

In order to answer some of these questions and contradictions we must plunge beneath the surface of ethnography in a more interpretive mode. I suggest that we may approach a deeper understanding of the culture we have studied through the notions of penetration and limitation.

'Penetration' is meant to designate impulses within a cultural form towards the penetration of the conditions of existence of its members and their position within the social whole but in a way not centred, essentialist or individualist. 'Limitation' is meant to designate those blocks, diversions and ideological effects which confuse and impede the full development and expression of these impulses. The rather clumsy term 'partial penetration' is meant to designate the interaction of these two terms in a concrete culture. Ethnography describes the field of play in which the impulses and limitations combine but cannot isolate them theoretically or show them separately. (Willis, 1977: 119)

This short statement says quite a lot about the paradoxes and ironies invoked by the subcultural approach.

Phil Cohen (1972) contributed a number of central tenets to the Birmingham subcultural approach in a lyrical paper on the shifting times in London's East End. He once again fixes the notion of subculture in relation to parent culture but he also realizes youth subcultures as a kind of index of the break-up and decay of their parent culture. Thus, he tells us: 'subculture, by definition, cannot break out of the contradiction derived from the parent culture; it merely transcribes its terms at a microsocial level and inscribes them in an imaginary set of conditions' (Cohen, in Gelder and Thornton, 1997: 96) and this accounts for the appearance of subcultures as closed systems. However, he continues:

But there is another reason. Apart from its particular, thematic contradiction, all subcultures share a general contradiction which is inherent in their very existence. Subculture invests the weak points in the chain of socialization between the family/school nexus and integration into the work process which marks the resumption of the patterns of the parent culture for the next generation. But subculture is also a compromise solution of two contradictory needs: the need to create and express *autonomy and difference* from parents and, by extension, their culture and the need to maintain the security of existing ego defenses and the *parental identifications* which support them. For the initiates the subculture provides a means of 'rebirth' without having to undergo the pain of symbolic death. (ibid.)

There are strong resonances with Willis here. Subcultures marked the younger generations' attempt to gain meaning and cohesion in the face of their parent (working-class) culture instancing fragmentation and a lack of solidarity and identity. The new conceptual territory provides a new set of meanings and identity formations but it has no critical role in redressing the conditions of the parent culture's decline. It is essentially passive in political terms – and here we note a contradiction with Hebdige.

Subcultures as Specifically Working-Class Phenomena

One final, and important point to emerge from Cohen's work is about the very specificity of subcultures. They are not analytical choices, they are what they are, both empirical and political realities:

> A distinction must be made between subcultures and delinquency. Many criminologists talk of delinquent subcultures. In fact, they talk about anything that is not middle-class culture as subculture. From my point of view, I do not think the middle class produces subcultures, for subcultures are produced by a dominant culture, not by a dominated culture. (ibid.: 97)

From this highly selective snapshot of studies emanating from the Birmingham group we note a range of similarities including the neo-Marxist transformations in the study of ideology, which we have considered at some length, a dedication to the issue of image and representation, largely through the notion of style, and an overwhelming sense that subcultures speak more than they say, they represent or are symbolic of bigger issues within the social process. It is on this last issue that the Birmingham contributors also begin to differ, the political significance of this form of representation was, and remains, a highly contested point. Subcultural theorists of all persuasions must be cautious not to exaggerate the concept, which is at one level no more than a gathering device, into the form of an empirical certainty which can serve to ghettoize and contain the naughty, the deviant and the non-normative or to over-emphasize mundane youthful posturing into the form of concerted (yet unconscious) political activism. Birmingham gave working-class youth back its agency, re-wrote its headlines and then reined it back in with ever more subtle forms of theoretic control.

Post-Birmingham, the concept of subculture remains popular in student dissertations, perhaps as a way of focusing on issues close to their own interests and immediate experience with an air of authority and supported by a respectable tradition. However, it is an arena little revisited by mainstream work within the tradition except as a vehicle to expose the lifestyle of nightlife, that is the twilight explosion of 'clubbing' beyond the Manchester Hacienda. Sarah Thornton (1995) produced a thoughtful and articulate account of what she coined as 'clubculture' with a perspective nearly twenty years evolved from Hebdige. For her, the political dimension of youth-ful leisure practice is far removed from the political and far more to do with lifestyle and patterns of consumption. Her concept of 'subcultural capital' openly derived from Bourdieu's concept of 'cultural capital' is similarly depoliticized and is more to do with a floating yet competitive aesthetic of taste which creates classifications and even hierarchies but is yet wholly unrelated to power. Bourdieu, through his interests in education as both a system of pedagogy but also a system of selection, was concerned that schools and society assess you on things they do not teach you. And the things they do not teach you are contained within the cultural capital that the dominant classes pass on as a form of inheritance which ensures their social and cultural reproduction. Thornton, on the other hand, is concerned with a far more transitory 'habitus' which provides a delicacy of taste (in relation to media imaging, fashion and self-presentation) which is wholly contained within the precincts of the club and carries no weight beyond that location:

> A critical difference between subcultural capital (as I explore it) and cultural capital (as Bourdieu develops it) is that the media are a primary factor governing the circulation of the former. Several writers have remarked upon the absence of television and radio from Bourdieu's theories of cultural hierarchy ... I would argue that it is impossible to understand the distinctions of youth subcultures without some systematic investigation of their media consumption. From within the economy of subcultural capital the media is not simply another symbolic good or marker of distinction ... but a network crucial to the definition and distribution of cultural knowledge. (Thornton, in Gelder and Thornton, 1997: 203)

A further short-lived and fairly insignificant cluster of work occurred through the aegis of the Manchester Institute of Popular Culture, mostly through the direction of Steve Redhead (1997). This was further attempt to re-politicize and properly evaluate popular culture but appeared needlessly over-burdened with the intricacies of 'Northern soul', 'DJs', 'raves' and 'football'. It was hard to discern a lasting theoretical framework.

This brings us more or less up to the present day. This book now concludes with a further analysis of my idea of the fragmentation of the social. All the excursions into subcultural theory and research previously considered are now placed on a problematic gradient, both in relation to modernity's project but also the purpose of sociology itself.

SEVEN Conclusion
Identity and Dispersion

What I trust we have achieved so far is a socially, and sociologically, contexted history of the idea of 'subculture'. However, this has not been a neutral appraisal of a widely accepted or generally applicable concept or analytic tool from the sociologist's tool-box. As we have seen, subculture is an idea with a highly restricted currency. I have set out to describe the inevitable constraints that the invocation of subculture, as an explanatory device, places upon the social world. I have also tried to show the equally inevitable, and mostly intended, consequences of the application of the concept in any piece of theory or sociological research. The idea of subculture has radical political dimensions and purposes and these, as we have seen, can stem from either progressive or reactionary political sentiments. The concept can be employed to valorise the underdog, radicalize the dispossessed, give voice to the inarticulate but equally to marginalize and contain the deviant or non-mainstream. It can and it does all of these things to different degrees according to the theorist's intent but also, and ironically, all of these things as well, despite the theorist's intent:

Although, or perhaps because, the term 'subculture' has been used by anthropologists and sociologists in a variety of ways and contexts, it contains much ambiguity. There is a reasonable degree of consensus in its use among sociologists, but other social scientists and psychologists may be less familiar with its implications. The prefix 'sub' refers only to a sub-category of culture, a part of a whole; it does not necessarily indicate derogation unless a particular subculture is viewed as undesirable by the members of the dominant or a contrary value system. For analytical purposes, the sociologist uses the term without a value judgement. (Wolfgang and Ferracuti, 1967: 95)

There, we could hardly have anticipated more conceptual confusion, even in a description of confusion.

The Paradox of Subcultural Theory

The idea of a subculture appears then, to be not just of limited usage but also shot through with paradox. Let us briefly revisit some of the examples we have previously explored. Parsons's corralling of deviance, in the forms of crime or political radicalism, as if they formed subcultures, puts such courses of action outside of the going order. However, it also establishes and confirms the alterity of such action and the real threat that it presents to the stability of that very order. In a similar manner, but inversely, the Chicago scholars' localized and spatial ethnographies wield an equally double-edged sword. Their exhaustive exposures of the routine everyday 'subcultural' practices of, for example, ghetto people, criminal gangs or hobos, proscribes their 'difference from' in a manner that makes it difficult for us to conceive of either the will, or the device, that would achieve the reintegration of such groups from their current state of marginalization. Indeed, the marginalization is, if anything, enhanced by their description through the idea of a 'subculture'. Likewise, the Birmingham CCCS group, though radical and liberationist in their intent, incidentally served to normalize youth reaction and protest in post-war Britain by rendering it fully intelligible through fashioning it into specific and bounded 'subcultures'. Beyond this analytical capture they then went on to ascribe such youthful agitation 'grown-up' political purposes, justified through a new theory of ideology. This latter analytical trope becomes understandable when seen in the context of the then current ideas of an American 'New Proletariat' informed by the works and teaching of Marcuse and Angela Davis in California, or, indeed, the British 'New Left' guided by Stuart Hall, but just how far did it correspond to the lived reality of those groups of adolescents? Finally, we might ask, rather pessimistically, has subcultural theory subsequently evolved into anything more than a desire to espouse pluralism and demonstrate an eager appreciation of popular culture? Well, perhaps not, but the history of the concept 'subculture' tells us more than this.

I wish to be clear, it is not my purpose in this conclusion to attempt to salvage the idea of subculture, to provide a late apologia nor to indicate new directions for future research. In one sense, what might be deduced from my argument throughout this work is that the concept never really had any mileage, in anybody's hands. In fact it might be suggested that the concept served merely as a distraction or a cul de sac in the development of sociological theory. In another sense, however, what has gone before can be read as saying that subculture, as an idea, has always signalled or marked out the limits of sociological reason. As such, the implementation of the concept, through various modes over the last century, are all expressions of those limitations. This status is not specific to the idea of a subculture, but subculture is one of the ways in which social theorists either fail to or simply avoid explaining the social in terms of the social. Looking to the larger issue, then, we might suggest that such limits as are revealed when we employ concepts such as subculture may in turn stand as instances or perhaps symptoms of an enfeebling of modernity's project, as expressed through sociology.

Subculture and Modernity's Project

But what might this mean? I am not suggesting that theorists have employed the idea of a subculture as a reflexive and self-conscious icon of modernity's exhaustion. Far from it, the idea has largely been employed as a convenience; as a place from which to stop theorizing. The invocation of the designation 'subculture' is a strategy that the theorist can adopt in order to give up on commonality and integration to focus on difference and diffusion. And this movement from the general to the particular, the macro to the micro, has been a trend much applauded in certain areas of sociology from the 1970s onwards. The confrontations between systems theory, structural Marxisms and phenomenology and the action frame of reference beginning in the late 1960s were all evidence of this shift and of a new 'perspectivalism'.

Viewed from a different position, subcultural ning, particularly in the hands of the Chicago School and 'I olt Parsons, can be seen as exercising precisely one of modernity s strategies, that is, to develop a changing consciousness about space. Modernity's initiative, among other things, sought out and discovered new worlds' which in turn implied the discovery of new and different peoples. The modern thinker became an explorer and an ethnologist. Likewise subcultural studies showed us ways of life and sides of the city that were strange, perhaps even shocking. New peoples, discoveries of new ways of life, inevitably impact on visions of future utopian societies and universal notions of the 'good' (and sociological theories of *society*). The politics of modernity foretells the politics of subcultural theory, the explorer, the discoverer, either emancipates or conquers; or most usually emancipates through conquering – what we refer to as colonization! All of the paradoxes of subcultural study, considered above, are contained by homology within this model of modernity. The scale of the geographical canvas is different but the spatial metaphors remain wholly appropriate across both contexts. Note Gouldner here, picking up this colonial drive while commenting on the neo-Chicagoan School of subcultural deviancy theory: '[it] expresses the satisfaction of a Great White Hunter who has bravely risked the perils of the urban jungle to bring back the exotic specimen' (1973: 37). What continued intellectual exploration, within this mode, reveals is ever newer versions of identity and difference, all of which confound established versions of commonality. In one sense, this is what Kuhn (1970) implied when he spoke of the 'anomalies' which at some point can no longer be contained within the old paradigm. We can respond to such revelations of anomaly through difference in a variety of ways. Essentially we can seek to hide or incorporate the anomalies by understating their disruption to the model, we can lament the past and the inappropriate view of consensus and celebrate difference (perhaps by letting a 'hundred flowers grow', the postmodern polysemy), or we might treat the preponderant vision, or paradigm, as the socio-historically located construct that it inevitably is and look to reform a view of the social that is more appropriate to current conditions. Again, subculture sits uncomfortably within these possibilities and can be used in any way and can therefore be read, paradoxically, in any way. Subculture tends mostly, however, to be employed to instance fragmentation and dispersion, it provides the medium within which the hundred flowers might grow. Durkheim, at the turn of the nineteenth century, had propounded a holistic theory of a solidaristic society that was also a reality *sui generis*. But even he noticed that solidarity and consensus and integration were far from 'total' realities and that, for example, crime existed in all societies, as we considered in Chapter 2. He did not therefore abandon his theory of solidarity, but instead, through his ideas of the 'normal' and the 'pathological' and the 'sacred' and the 'profane', he included crime as a normal, functional element of any contemporary world. Crime tested the boundaries of the 'centre' and thus strengthened them. Crime was not to be taken as a discrete society or subculture in isolation, it lived in a dynamic and therefore interactive mode with other functioning features of the society.

Subculture and the Decay of Modernity

Many commentators have noted the anachronistic tendency in modernity's central thrust. The happy, altruistic, integrated, fully expressed and fully realized human being in the Enlightenment vision has become gradually mugged by history. In the twentieth century we have witnessed a decline in, or even collapse of, faith in the possibilities of emancipation through progress. Also in decline is the belief in the liberating potential of science. In fact, the accompanying advance of technology through modernity has not extended humankind's plasticity into perfection but rather into horror through strategies and implements of mass destruction. Comparative study reveals that time has done little to socialize Thomas Hobbes's species being and, perhaps, ideas like 'subculture' are attempts to come to grips with this shortfall. It is possible that some group or groups will stage a revival. In the nineteenth century we saw the development of Marx's thought from Hegel's view of the master–slave relationship. Marx over-invested in the heroic possibilities of the proletariat to transform themselves and thus the whole structuring of social relationships, but where is such a group now? – women, black people, queer folk, hybrids, cyborgs or even Hebdige's youthful subcultures? However, the election of the difference that constitutes any subculture as a 'way forward' or a 'resistance' or a 'brave new world' is often unbalanced. It does not, it would seem, consist in applying the same criteria, the same critique, to the subculture as it does to the 'old', 'mainstream' or 'dominant' culture. Stan Cohen saw this in much of the Birmingham work at an early stage:

> The subculture is observed and decoded, its creativity celebrated and its political limitations acknowledged – and then the critique of the social order constructed. But while this critique of stems from moral absolutism, the subculture itself is treated in the language of cultural relativism. Those same values of racism, sexism, chauvinism, compulsive masculinity anti-intellectualism, the slightest traces of which are condemned in bourgeois culture, are treated with a deferential care ... when they appear in the subculture. (1980: xxvii)

Maybe we have moved too fast, our conclusion has led off too quickly. We are beginning to embrace the utter relativism of postmodern without the foreplay of modernity's tradition. Let us look at the broader historical picture. Let us regard sociology as the philosophy of modernity and then inquire if, indeed, it has been outstripped by, completed within or simply failed to regenerate in the face of the historical process. It was the new moral science, sociology, as conceived in Europe, that would bind the contemporary and emergent society together. Particularly so in the face of the ravages and stresses that were being wrought through modernity's other more concrete manifestations, such as industrialization, the division of labour, urbanization, capitalism and bureaucracy and all of the consequent corrosive vectors that they were instilling in the social system, such as anomie, alienation and neurosis.

The development of sociology confronted us with the problem of a new reality – that is, 'society' as a thing to be studied, not just to take part in. Experientially, being in society is difficult enough, but as an object of understanding it has always presented inscrutable difficulties. So just what then is society? Is it synonymous with culture, and can it be readily subdivided and conveniently broken down into subcultures without destroying its purpose, sociology's intent? And is this really a move in language?

> From the point of view of what might be called social hermeneutics, the question of language as such relates to the dispersion of meaning into the monological sub-cultural communities characteristic of modernity, and to the registering and explicit recognition – enshrined in the principle of difference – of this state of late-modernity. (Heywood, 1997: 192)

For the greater part of the last century we were content to understand the social through conceptual vehicles such as 'order', 'systems', and shared norms and values. Now these devices served well and enabled us to sustain a feeble idea of society as being rather like the flat earth with a centre, a cohesive force and strict edges. Social theorists routinely talked about normative conduct and deviant conduct. However, this was an important yet difficult distinction to draw, largely because it was a moral distinction not an empirical one (just as the designation 'sub-' might be). Increasingly it dawned on us that our simple model was unsupported by life itself. Society did not rest on an even base, there were folds and subterranean tendrils moving from part to part. The parts no longer interrelated so easily, there was no obvious harmony or agreement, but instead competition, difference and divergence. For most of the time, we might suppose, most of the people think and believe and act in broadly complementary ways, but some of them do not. How do we explain those who do not? Well, mostly through ideas like 'subculture'. Yet to do so is to abandon those who we suppose 'do not'.

Subculture and Postmodernity

But our late-modern problem as social theorists begins somewhere else. It is likely that contemporary society's multiple manifestations are now in such flux and a state of constant proliferation that our real problem resides in attempting to theorize what most of us mostly do, that is what we previously referred to as the 'centre'.

> The romance of the marginal is to be found throughout postmodern cultural politics. Work on youth style and subculture, such as Dick Hebdige's, derives its authority from this embrace of the marginal. Hebdige takes up as an embodiment of the subcultural subject the French writer Jean Genet, who is, he says, 'a subculture in himself'. Genet retains his position as a thief, liar and outsider *par excellence*, and it is his refusal to be contaminated by the dominant orders that preserves intact the subversive potential of his marginal condition ... This form of subcultural study takes its place within a cultural/critical frame which explores the possibilities of inverting conventional mappings and the distribution of power. (Connor, 1989: 228–9)

Because of the growing difficulties in identifying the centre, the mainstream social theory now had to resort to other devices such as solidarity, culture, community, even subculture, to express pockets of agreement and to reaffirm our faith in the collective life. The discipline, having evolved in part through the competition between theoretical perspectives, shifted through a series of meta-paradigms which were regarded sequentially as the 'linguistic turn', the 'reflexive turn', the 'cultural turn' and the 'visual turn', as we discussed in Chapter 1. This macro-conceptual evolution was not just one that was driven by an individual sense of intellectual purpose. The society itself was moving more and more rapidly and the *Zeitgeist* was shifting, or adapting, with equal speed. The swift, and rather sudden, transition of ideas through post-structuralism in the 1980s pronounced the death of what Lyotard described as the 'grand narratives' of modernity:

> Modernity begins with the deligitimation of traditional knowledge by science. The inception of *post*modernity is marked, then, by the deligitimation of science; for Lyotard, it has now been widely accepted – a constitutive feature of postmodernity itself – that the language game of science can only be legitimated from within. This is another way of expressing the continuing effects within social and cultural theory of the linguistic turn. (Heywood, 1997: 44)

This, essentially, meant that the stories that had sustained the Enlightenment vision were themselves opened up for investigation and seen to contain unexpressed interests and power relations, but, more than this, they were found to be simply no longer compatible with the lived experience of contemporary life. One such grand narrative was the central sociological idea of 'society' itself. The sociologists' binding concept became a victim of the discipline's new forms of understanding and, in many senses, we might suggest that such an occurrence had been on a gradient throughout the development of social theory. The social, a totalizing concept, has steadily relinquished its analytical and causal power. Now, the consequences of such a break in faith or, what I have described in the title of this book as a 'fragmentation of the social', has been a de-traditionalization, a dispersion and a gradual loss of accountability. And worse still, an acceptance of that state of affairs as normal. Any knowledge of human relations has now been cast loose onto the vagaries of a range of more micro, more flexible and more dedicatedly unstable loci such as 'standpoints' and 'identity politics'. The idea of a subculture can be understood simultaneously as part of this problem and also as a rearguard attempt to establish islands of social stability.

At the same time as, and because of, these epistemological changes, the institutional context of the intellectual life changed. The academy erupted into the era of the post-, with post-history; post-feminism; post-colonialism; post-nationalism and, overarching them all, the spectre of the 'postmodern'. Tangible metaphors of the social no longer seemed viable and our languages of order gave way to new geographies of social space, many of which appeared entirely cognitive. What remained, however, was a lingering, and real, sense of limits, which I have considered elsewhere through the notion of 'transgression' (Jenks, 2003). Though diffuse and ill-defined the limits, the margins, now took on a most important role in describing and defining the centre. Beyond the limits: be they classificatory, theoretical or even moral, there remained asociality or chaos but ever more vivid and in greater proximity. However, nor should we forget the reflexive power of the limits and our systems of classification. They are not neutral or descriptive, rather, they capture the world in their own projected image and in so doing they save it from its randomness, for better or worse:

> Culture ... may be seen as a source of potential meaning structures that actors inherit. Subcultures, by their very existence, suggest that there are alternative forms of cultural expression which reflect a cultural plurality of a culture which seems on superficial examination to dominate the members

of a society. Culture has several levels: the historical level of ideas, the level of values, the level of meaning and its effect on art, signs and symbols. There is also the process of material production and the symbolic and material effects of artefacts on cultures. Finally, there is the personal, dynamic element of human action and the way it is interpreted between actors. Subcultures exist where there is some form of organized and recognized constellation of values, behaviour and action which are responded to as different from the prevailing set of norms. (Brake, 1985: 8–9)

At the risk of obscuring our particular topic 'subculture', but also with the central purpose of ensuring that it is properly explained and situated in the unfolding history of ideas, we will now take an informative diversion into the realm of the postmodern. This re-routing should, I hope, demonstrate the outcome of the analytical slippery slope that I believe the concept 'subculture' has abetted.

The Acceleration of the Post-

In the space of twenty years postmodernism has grown from the status of a mood to that of a reality; or at least a reality-in-thought. Its compulsive empire, projected forward by the tenuous and somewhat neurotic principles of self-decentring, the unrecognizability of priority, and committed instability, has expanded in step with this elevation in status. What was once a localized, and healthy, concern with the limits of the Modernist trajectory in fine art and architecture has grown beyond arrogance into hubris, and mounted a critique of modern life and, more particularly, the forms of knowledge and value that support and sustain such living.

Postmodernism is not discipline-specific. Rather, it is a mind-set and takes recognizable form either as an external attack on the methods and values of our time, or, simultaneously, as a spontaneous, intentional and internally generated symptom of our time. A phenomenon of this magnitude and scope is worthy of our concern: it affects our conceptions of society, it challenges, undermines and perhaps changes our conceptions of society and culture, it may even constitute our sense of social relations and culture. Or it may provide a need and a disposition to address the collectivity (and other such 'questionable' notions) through more specific and factionalized concepts like subculture. Such a knee-jerk reaction may be intelligible in the face of certain elitist and hierarchical formulations like T.S. Eliot's, where culture includes:

all the characteristic activities and interests of a people ... (thus for the English) ... Derby Day, Henley Regatta, Cowes, the twelfth of August, the cup final, the dog races, the pin table, the dart board, Wensleydale cheese, boiled cabbage cut into sections, beetroot in vinegar, nineteenth century Gothic churches and the music of Elgar. (Eliot, 1948: 17)

But not all sociological thinking is premised upon or predisposed to adopt such assumptions. More than this, we are witnessing no simple knee-jerk reaction. What has occurred is a distrust and a dissatisfaction with the state of the modern world, its politics and their failure to deliver, but also with its forms of knowledge.

Postmodernism steadfastly refuses to offer alternative ways of knowing, more timely or appropriate ways of confronting and appreciating the 'new'. Rather, it insinuates itself into all discourse, it undermines existing epistemologies, and seeks to reduce and disempower explanations that it regards as premised upon the wholly privileged discourses, unlike its own! Drawing on the deconstruction inherent in much post-structuralist thought Baudrillard (1983), an early leading figure, has occupied the site between the signifier and the signified and justified it in the manner of a diagnosis, and even celebration, of the entropic tendencies of our time. For Lyotard (1984) the difference between moral and political positions is as significant as the play of language games, and the theorist, the self, derives from the intersection and interface between these games – the *differend* – the synapses through which the various messages flow. The struggle over the sign is clearly begun, and there are no prior claims that can justify their authority. The rule is that the rules on which the system was composed no longer apply. Within this swath social theory stands or falls (Bauman, 1992; Callinicos, 1989; Jenks, 1993b; O'Neill, 1995), as does the concept of society itself.

Although the idea of postmodernism appears artfully to elude definition, a bold summation of its disconcerted elements has been attempted by Hebdige. His definition has not been selected at random but precisely because of the reasons that built many of the arguments here in his wake, he is a primary exponent of the modern concept of 'subculture':

Postmodernism – we are told – is neither a homogeneous entity nor a consciously directed 'movement'. It is instead a space, a 'condition', a 'predicament', an *aporia*, an 'unpassable path' – where competing intentions, definitions, and effects, diverse social and intellectual tendencies and lines of force converge and clash. When it becomes possible for people to describe as 'postmodern' the decor of a room, the design of a building, the diagesis of a film, the construction of a record, or a scratch video, a television commercial, or an arts documentary, or the intertextual relations between them, the layout of a page in a fashion magazine or critical journal, an anti-teleological tendency within epistemology, the attack on the metaphysics of presence, a general attenuation of feeling, the collective chagrin and morbid projections of a post War generation of baby boomers confronting disillusioned middle age, the predicament of 'reflexivity', a group of rhetorical tropes, a proliferation of surfaces, a new phase in commodity fetishism, a fascination for images, codes and styles, a process of cultural, political or existential fragmentation and/or crisis, the 'decentring' of the subject, an 'incredulity towards metanarratives', the replacement of unitary power axes by a plurality of power/discourse formations, the 'implosion of meaning', the collapse of cultural hierarchies, the dread engendered by the threat of nuclear self-destruction, the decline of the university, the functioning and effects of the new miniaturized technologies, broad societal and economic shifts into a 'media', 'consumer', or 'multinational' phase, a sense (depending on who you read) of placelessness (Jameson on the Bonnaventura Hotel) or the abandonment of placelessness (e.g. Kenneth Frampton's 'critical regionalism') or (even) a generalised substitution of spatial for temporal coordinates – when it becomes possible to describe all these things as 'postmodern' (or more simply using a current abbreviation, as 'post' or 'very post') then it's clear that we are in the presence of a buzzword. (Hebdige, in Jenks, 1993a: 70–1)

The story behind postmodernism, although it resists the narrative form, is about the end of another and greater story that we have already alluded to. The concluding tale is that which was written by the Enlightenment. The Enlightenment established a set of typical characters, with typical motives and a shared goal, that is to say that it provided the 'grand' narrative form for the history of modernity. Reason was to triumph over faith, humankind was to become the measure of all things, nature was to be quelled and put to the service of humankind, and time was to be measured in terms of a transition from darkness into the light, a transition and an implicit theory of moral evolution that came to be known as *progress*. The centrality of humankind and, following Descartes, cognitive subjectivism, when linked to the institutionalized mode of reason that we call science was the methodology of this master plan. However, as history has shown us, the self-appointed claims of the methodology, those to objectivity, and the ideological insulation of its practitioners, in the form of value-neutrality, have created an accelerative moral vacuum. World wars, techniques and technologies of mass extermination and a market-led programme of subsequently polluting productivity have all weighed in the deficit column to offset the gains in health, income, enlightenment, democratization and overall quality of life. Major events, along with the cumulative effects of minor irritations, appear to have shaken our faith in 'society' as a state of being, as a home and as a source of causality.

Apart from the more obvious economic, technological and political changes that had brought our present circumstances into being there were also two grand philosophical moments that had predicted their moral consequences. As we have just stated, the Enlightenment was a prime instigator with its insistence on the ultimate perfectibility of human kind – a goal that was to be achieved by privileging calculative reason. The second was Nietzsche's intervention. The Enlightenment ideal has meant three things: (1) that we have come to confuse change with progress; (2) that we have experimented with human excellence through various flawed political policies; and, finally, (3) that we have become intolerant if not incredulous towards 'deviant' behaviour (that is, behaviour that we suppose most of us are not doing most of the time). Nietzsche's shattering revelation about God's demise, on the other hand, has given rise to three different but contributory processes: (1) it has removed certainty; (2) it has mainstreamed the re-evaluation of values; and, finally, (3) it has released control over infinity. Nietzsche, the philosopher of the postmodern, had, it can be argued, predicted and applauded the advent of this age of negative alchemy. His philosophical stylistics were, there is no doubt, concerned with morality – its redundancy and disassembly, to be more precise. Nietzsche made a series of pronouncements concerning the topic and purpose of philosophy and the weaknesses and degenerations that its conventional forms had wrought. Most serious and lasting is that uttered in the allegorical guise of *Zarathustra*, the pilgrim of postmodernity. His mantra, 'God is dead', he declares repeatedly. Now this is no simple sociological observation concerning the secularization of modern Western society, although it may be superstructural to such a phenomenon. What the philosopher is announcing is the collapse of the centre and the consequent decentralization of value. He simultaneously undermines all hitherto existing belief systems which, of course, strikes at the collective life. We can recall from Chapter 2 the symbolic elision that was artfully employed in Durkheim's later works. In contradistinction to all of those turn of the century metaphors from social theory stressing 'integration', 'solidarity', 'community', 'structure', 'instrumentality' and 'culture' itself, in sum, the language of *unification*, Nietzsche is recommending *dispersion*. The survival of the human spirit rests no longer in the hands of collectivities but in the affirmation of the new warrior, the individual in the incarnation of the *Übermensch* (the superman). Man must escape from the protective politics of order into an affirmation of life as 'the will to power'. Herewith are the seeds of our new cultural critic. But through the practice of the postmodern we can also excavate the trace elements of the subcultural:

> If we move quarter of a century ahead, to Nietszche in the 1880s, we will find very different prejudices, allegiances and hopes, yet a surprisingly similar voice and feeling for modern life. For Nietzsche, as for Marx, the currents of modern history were ironic and dialectical: thus Christian ideals of the soul's integrity and the will to truth had come to explode Christianity itself. The results were the traumatic events that Nietzsche called 'the death of God' and the 'advent of nihilism'. Modern mankind found itself in the midst of a great absence and emptiness of values and yet, at the same time, a remarkable abundance of possibilities. (Berman, 1982: 21)

Postmodernism, after Nietzsche, offers no millennial philosophy searching for the 'good' society in a stable recognizable form – such is the discourse of Marx, Weber and Durkheim, the 'conventional' theorists all, in their various ways, relating and responding to Hegel's optimistic vision of the historical process. There is no process for Nietzsche, no tradition, no *entelechy*: his *telos* is in the instability of process. The power of the will and the constant revaluation of values are the 'good', in themselves. No 'end' point can, nor should, be envisaged, no new or improved set of values is the purpose of being, but only the challenge of convention. If there can be no end, then the process built on the 'grand narrative', 'myth', or 'values' of history is nothing more than an eternal return of circumstances, values, people and things. We must seek out moments of challenge, interruption, opposition and resistance.

Nietzsche's intuitive, anti-deductionist, anti-rationalist ideas challenge the classical tradition of philosophy and fly in the face of the metaphysical project, a knowledge of being, a vision of history. All metaphysical systems and ethical paradigms, for him, disguise assumptions and interests that are committed to the preservation of a weak stasis, the stagnation of the will and the triumph of mediocrity over the strength of creative being. Following in the wake of this violent assault on the social ethic is the clamouring Babel that postmodernism designates 'polysemy', the many voices within a culture waiting to be heard all with an equivalence and a right, ranging from the oppressed to, simply, the previously unspoken:

What is distinctive and remarkable about the voice that Marx and Nietzsche share is not only its breathless pace, its vibrant energy, its imaginative richness, but also its fast and drastic shifts in tone and inflection, its readiness to turn on itself, to question and negate all it has said, to transform itself into a great range of harmonic or dissonant voices, and to stretch itself beyond its capacities into an endlessly wider range, to express and grasp a world where everything is pregnant with its contrary and 'all that is solid melts into air'. This voice resonates at once with self-discovery and self-mockery, with self-delight and self-doubt. It is a voice that knows pain and dread, but believes in its power to come through. Grave danger is everywhere, and may strike at any moment, but not even the deepest wounds can stop the flow and overflow of its energy. It is ironic and contradictory, polyphonic and dialectical, denouncing modern life in the name of values that modernity itself has created, hoping – often against hope – that the modernities of tomorrow and the day after tomorrow will heal the wounds that wreck the modern men and women of today. (Berman, 1982: 23)

Identity Politics

A quarter of a century ago we discussed 'society' as a reality with confidence, as recently as 1990 we considered ideas like a 'common culture' without caution, even within left-wing discourse from R.H. Tawney to Paul Willis. Today, in the wake of a series of debates we cannot even pronounce such holisms without fear of intellectual reprisals on the basis of epistemological imperialism. 'Identity politics' has become a new currency with different, and increasingly minority, groups claiming a right to speak and equivalence of significance. Perpetually fresh questions are raised about the relationship between the core of social life and the periphery; the centre and the margins; identity and difference, the normal and the deviant, and the possible rules that could conceivably bind us into a collectivity. Now this is the conceptual territory occupied by ideas such as 'subculture'. They mark out difference, they hold it tight, and they give meaning to it. Half a century ago, Albert Cohen concluded a foundational paper on the theory of subcultures within his book on delinquents as follows:

A complete theory of subcultural differentiation would state more precisely the conditions under which subcultures emerge and fail to emerge, and would state operations for predicting the content of subcultural solutions ... the completion of this theory must await a great deal more of hard thinking and research. (Cohen, 1955: 72)

His point, not at its strongest here, preserves the ontological status of subcultures as just 'there' and invites us to think harder about what generates the conditions of their differentiation. But if we read him in a more modern, more phenomenological way, then the questions he raises become epistemological, not ontological. They are now not questions about the factual origins of these social objects 'subcultures', rather, they are analytical questions about the reasons why and the devices through which the theorist elected to realize the world in subcultural terms. In other words, and to paraphrase, why does the deviancy or youth cultural theorist wish to constitute their object of attention as something discontinuous with the centre, the society, the common culture? At what point does the theorist decide that the interests within their designated subculture can no longer be contained within a more totalizing concept, and what then have subcultures got in common other than their differentiation? And, of course, the reasons are never simply analytical, they are political and moral and thus paradoxical.

These kinds of concerns have always been raised but in liminal zones within the culture such as the avant garde; in the context of radical political movements such as anarchism and situationism; and counter-cultural traditions in creative practice like Dada and Surrealism. Yet theoretical devices to contrive or generate differentiation may produce an alteration but without an identifiable positivity, they do not produce an alterity. This has been a problem of the Western avant-garde throughout the twentieth century. If their transgressions and differentiations produce an alterity, it does not necessarily compromise the past. Such questions have now moved from the liminal zones into more mainstream discourse. Berman (1985), after Marx, announced 'all that which is solid melts into air' and, following the prophetic words of the poet Yeats, we have all become aware that 'the centre cannot hold'. A feeling of insecurity has entered into our consciousness, an insecurity concerning our relationships with others and concerning the ownership of our own desires. We are no longer sure on what basis we belong to another being ... or group!

The question of modernity confronts us unavoidably with the relation between Language, our languages, and the 'present', our 'presence', the 'presence' of things and others for us: we are faced with how to re-present 'the times' in which we live and with what 'it is' to be 'timely' in such re-presentation. It confronts us, as Rimbaud has shown us, with the problem of the relevance of what we bring, carry over and forward, from the past of the language we learn from others, the language of the past, the artistic tradition, to our relation to the 'present'. The experience, the diagnosis, the dilemma of modernity seem to begin with this refusal of what Tradition delivers us as the expected, indeed the required conventions. (Phillipson, 1985: 29)

This present state of uncertainty and flux within our culture raises fundamental questions concerning the categories of the normal and the pathological when applied to action or social institutions. Such periods of instability, as we are now experiencing, tend to test and force issues of authority and tradition – truth and certainty are up for question. Clearly the 1960s provide another recent example of such a febrile epoch and it was this epoch that gave rise to many of the youthful configurations that became the 'subcultures' of the British National Deviancy Symposium, the New Deviancy and the Birmingham Centre. But within that historical context, the politics were clearer, they were Marxists and anti-establishment. It would seem that instability and uncertainty are experienced today in peculiarly privatized forms that rarely extend beyond ourselves or our immediate circle. Far from a fear of freedom, we now appear to espouse a fear of collectivity, we have become wary of seeking out commonality with others. The vociferous politics of our time are thus 'identity politics', and the response to dominant conditions is often poetic.

It is only by having a strong sense of the 'together' that we can begin to understand and account for that which is outside, at the margins or, indeed, that which defies the consensus. The contemporary rebel is left with neither utopianism nor nihilism, but rather loneliness. However, we need to affirm that human experience is the constant experience of limits, perhaps because of the absolute finitude of death; this is a point made forcefully by Bataille (1985). Constraint is a constant experience in our action, it needs to be to render us social. Interestingly enough, however, the limits to our experience and the taboos that police them, are never simply imposed from the outside; rather, limits to behaviour are always personal responses to moral imperatives that stem from the inside. This means that concepts like 'subculture' can be seen as ways of containment, as a kind of cognitive wrapping paper and string with which to bundle up clusters of deviance, criminality, ethnicity, poverty or just generations. 'Adolescents are grouped together by adults and defined as a problem, and yet we must ask ourselves whether this problem refers to something in the adolescent, or whether it is making a statement about society' (Friedenburg, quoted in Brake, 1985: 1).

Conclusion

Where, then, does this leave 'subculture', the concept we started out from? My sense is that the idea has run its course. As a device in the hands of sociologists, or more recently the exponents of cultural studies, it has keenly avoided the difficulties that are presented when we attempt to explain elements of the social world in terms of society itself. Instead of addressing the difficulties that the idea of 'society' presents, the theorist rejects or leaves behind the grand, totalizing concept with an ideological justification in terms of the politics of today. What is occurring in this context is not so much a transition into post-modernity as a particularly twentieth-century version of anti-modernity. This amounts to little more than a giving-up on ideas, conversations, narratives or commitments that no longer seem to get the job done. Instead of resurrecting the social and attempting to include the emergent identities and differences, they are enabled to speak for themselves, without the constraints of collective inclusion, in the form of subcultures. Subcultures therefore emerge as the new times and places that people occupy, subcultures are the new sources of identity, subcultures are the new signifier of difference. The consequences of such theoretic action are not ultra-modern, they are retrogressive, nihilistic and utterly relativistic. They can be defended by no politic nor morality. It sounds exciting and liberal to designate youth as the flagship of the new dawn, it does not sound quite so appealing to relegate all naughty deviant behaviour to a stockade of pathology, distance and personal responsibility. What about the new folk devils, paedophiles, do they constitute a new subculture? Do they communicate on the Internet, do they have meetings, a shared language, a symbolic repertoire, a whole way of life or are they bank clerks, accountants, civil servants, fathers, citizens, athletes, and members of the Labour Party as well? Do we understand their dark inclinations better by expelling them from anything we claim to share or do we see better for placing them on a spectrum with our own behaviour and asking what it is about the 'society' that we all live in that enables and motivates their particular form of conduct? What about the people who always seem to live next door, who always play their music too loud, could they comprise a subculture – or are you the people who always seem to live next door?

Bibliography

Abbott, A. (1999) *Department and Discipline: Chicago School at One Hundred*, Chicago: University of Chicago Press.

Agger, B. (1992) *Cultural Studies as Critical Theory*, London: Falmer.

Alexander, J. (1988) *Durkheimian Sociology: Cultural Studies*. Cambridge: Cambridge University Press.

Alihan, M. (1938) *Social Ecology: A Critical Analysis*, New York: Columbia University Press.

Althusser, L. (1971) 'Ideological and repressive state apparatuses', in L. Althusser, *Lenin and Philosophy and Other Essays*, London: New Left Books.

Anderson, N. (1923) *The Hobo: The Sociology of the Homeless Man*, Chicago: University of Chicago Press.

Banks, O. (1968) *The Sociology of Education*, London: Batsford.

Baudrillard, J. (1983) *In the Shadow of the Silent Majorities*, New York: Semiotext(e).

Baudrillard, J. (1984) *Simulations*, New York: Semiotext(e).

Bauman, Z. (1988) 'Is there a postmodern sociology?', *Theory, Culture and Society*, 5 (2–3): 217.

Bauman, Z. (1992) *Intimations of Postmodernity*, London: Routledge.

Becker, H. (1963) *Outsiders*, New York: Free Press.

Bennett, T., Mercer, C. and Woollacott, J. (eds) (1981) *Popular Culture and Social Relations*, Milton Keynes: Open University Press.

Berman, M. (1985) *All That Is Solid Melts Into Air: The Experience of Modernity*, London: Verso.

Besant, W. (1882) *All Sorts and Conditions of Men*, republished Oxford: Oxford University Press (1997).

Blumer, H. (1969) *Symbolic Interactionism*, Eaglewood Cliffs, NJ: Prentice Hall.

Boggs, C. (1976) *Gramsci's Marxism*, London: Pluto Press.

Bourdieu, P. (1993) *The Field of Cultural Production*, Oxford: Polity Press.

Brake, M. (1980) *The Sociology of Youth Culture and Youth Subcultures*, London: Routledge.

Brake, M. (1985) *Comparative Youth Culture*, London: Routledge.

Burgess, R. (1986) *Sociology, Education and Schools*, London: Batsford.

Callinicos, A. (1982) *Is there a Future for Marxism?*, London: Verso.

Callinicos, A. (1989) *Against Postmodernism*, Cambridge: Polity.

Chaney, D. (1994) *The Cultural Turn: Scene-setting Essays on Contemporary Cultural History*, London: Routledge.

Cicourel, A. (1964) *Method and Measurement in Sociology*, New York: Free Press.

Clarke, J., Hall, S., Jefferson, T. and Roberts, B. (1981) 'Sub-cultures, cultures and class', in T. Bennett, C. Mercer and J. Woollacott (eds) *Popular Culture and Social Relations,* Milton Keynes: Open University Press.

Cohen, A. (1955) *Delinquent Boys*, New York: Free Press.

Cohen, P. (1972) 'Subcultural conflict and working-class community', in *Working Papers in Cultural Studies No. 2*, University of Birmingham Centre for Contemporary Cultural Studies.

Cohen, S. (1980) *Folk Devils and Moral Panics*, 2nd edn, London: Martin Robertson.

Connor, S. (1989) *Postmodernist Culture*, Oxford: Basil Blackwell.

Cooley, C.H. (1902) *Human Behavior and the Social Order*, New York: Charles Scribner's and Sons.

Dawe, A. (1970) 'The two sociologies', *British Journal of Sociology*, 21 (2): 207–218.

Downes, D. (1966) *The Delinquent Solution: A Study in Subcultural Theory*, London: Routledge.

Durkheim, E. (1964a) *The Division of Labour in Society*, New York: Free Press.

Durkheim, E. (1964b) The Rules of the Sociological Method, New York: Free Press.

Durkheim, E. (1971) *The Elementary Forms of the Religious Life*, London: Allen and Unwin.

Durkheim, E. (1974) *Sociology and Philosophy*, New York: Free Press.

Durkheim, E. (1992) *Professional Ethics and Civic Morals*, london: Routledge.

Durkheim, E. and Mauss, M. (1970) *Primitive Classification*, London: Routledge.

Eagleton, T. (1983) *Literary Theory: An Introduction*, Oxford: Blackwell.

Eliot, T.S. (1948) *Notes Towards a Definition of Culture*, New York: Harcourt.

Feyerabend, P. (1978) *Against Method*, London: Verso.

Foucault, M. (1979) 'On governmentality', *Ideology and Consciousness*, 6: 20–39.

Gelder, K. and Thompson, S. (eds) (1997a) *The Subcultures Reader*, London: Routledge.

Gelder, K. and Thornton, S. (eds) (1997b) 'General introduction', *The Subcultures Reader*, London: Routledge.

Gilroy, P. (1987) *There Ain't No Black in the Union Jack*, London: Unwin Hyman.

Gordon, M. (1947) 'The concept of the sub-culture and its application', *Social Forces,* 26 October.

Gouldner, A. (1970) *The Coming Crisis in Western Sociology*, London: Heinmann.

Gouldner, A. (1973) 'The sociologist as partisan', in *For Sociology*, London: Allen Lane.

Gramsci, A. (1971) 'Libero pensiero e pensiero libero', in *Il Grido del Popolo 15 June 1918*, Rome: Scritti Giovani.

Gramsci, A. (1973) *Selections from the Prison Notebooks*, London: Lawrence and Wishart.

Gramsci, A. (1975) *Quaderni del Carcere*, Torino: Einaudi.

Gurvich, G. (1957) *The Social Framework of Knowledge* (English Trans. 1971), Oxford: Blackwell.

Hall, S. (1981) 'Cultural studies: two paradigms', in T. Bennett, G. Martin, C.

Mercer and J. Woollacott, (eds), *Culture, Ideology and Social Process*, Milton Keynes: Open University amd London: Batsford.

Hall, S. and Jefferson, T. (1975) *Resistance Through Ritual*, London: Routledge.

Hargreaves, D. (1967) *Social Relations in the Secondary School*, London: Routlege.

Harris, K. (2001) 'Transgression and mundanity: the global extreme metal music scene', unpublished PhD thesis, University of London

Harvey, D. (1989) *The Condition of Postmodernity*, Oxford: Blackwell.

Hebdige, D. (1983) 'Posing. . . threats, striking. . . poses: youth, surveillance and display', *SubStance* 37/38: 63–88.

Hebdige, D. (1988) *Hiding in the Light*, London: Routledge.

Hebdige, D. (1993) 'A report on the Western Front: postmodernism and the "politics" of style', in C. Jenks (ed.), *Cultural Reproduction*, London: Routledge.

Heywood, I. (1997) *Social Theories of Art*, Basingstoke: Macmillan.

Hoggart, R. (1985) *The Uses of Literacy*, Harmondsworth: Penguin.

Hollis, M. (1977) *Models of Man*, Cambridge: Cambridge University Press.

Homans, G. (1948) *The Human Group*, London: Routledge.

Hutcheon, L. (1989) *The Politics of Postmodernism*, London: Routledge.

Jackson, P. and Marsden, D. (1962) *Education and the Working Class*, London: Routledge.

Jenks, C. (ed.) (1993a) *Cultural Reproduction*, London: Routledge.

Jenks, C. (1993b) *Culture*, London: Routledge.

Jenks, C. (ed.) (1995) *Visual Culture*, London: Routledge.

Jenks, C. (2003) *Transgression*, London: Routledge.

Johnson, R. (1983) 'What is cultural studies anyway', CCC stencilled paper No. 74.

Jordanova, L. (1994) 'The hand', in L. Taylor (ed.) *Visualizing Theory*, London: Routledge.

Kellner, D. (1988) 'Postmodernism as a social theory: some challenges and problems', *Theory, Culture and Society*, 5 (2-3): 239–69.

Kroker, A. and Cook, D. (1986) *The Postmodern Scene: Excremental Culture and Hyper-aesthetics*, New York: New World Perspectives.

Kluckhohn, C. and Kelley, W. (1962) 'The concept of culture' reprinted in C. Kluckhohn, *Culture and Behavior*, New York: Vintage Books.

Komarovsky, M. and Sargent, S. (1949) 'Research into subcultural influences upon personality', in S. Sargent and M. Smith (eds) *Culture and Personality*, New York: The Viking Fund.

Kuhn, T. (1970) *The Structure of Scientific Revolutions*, Chicago: Chicago University Press.

Lacey, C. (1970) *Hightown Grammar*, Manchester: Manchester University Press.

Lash, S. and Freidman, J. (eds) (1992) 'Subjectivity and modernity's other', in *Modernity and Identity*, Oxford: Blackwell.

Lee, A. (1945) 'Levels of culture as levels of social generalization', in *American Sociological Review*,10, August: 125–43.

Liebow, E. (1967) *Tally's Corner: A Study of Negro Streetcorner Men*, Boston: Little, Brown and Co.

Lukes, S. (1985) *Emile Durkheim: His Life and Works*, Stanford CA: Stanford University Press.

Lyotard, J-F. (1984) *The Postmodern Condition*, Manchester: Manchester

University Press.

Madge, J. (1963) *The Origins of Scientific Sociology*, London: Tavistock.

Maffesoli, M. (1996) *The Time of the Tribes: The Decline of Individualism in Mass Society*, London: Sage.

Maine, H. (1876) *Village Communities in the East and West*, London: John Murray.

Mayhew, H. (1950) *London's Underworld*, edited by P. Quennell, London: Spring Books.

McGuigan, J. (1992) *Cultural Populism*, London: Routledge.

McHale, D. (1987) *Postmodernist Fiction*, London: Methuen.

McHugh, P. (1971) 'On the failure of positivism', in J. Douglas, (ed.), *Understanding Everyday Life*, London: Routledge.

McLellan, D. (ed.) (1988) *Marxism: Essential Readings*, Oxford: Oxford University Press.

McRobbie, A. (1981) 'Settling accounts with subcultures: a feminist critique', in T. Bennett (ed.) *Culture, Ideology and Social Process*, London: Batsford.

McRobbie, A. and Garber, J. (1975) 'Girls and subculture', in S. Hall and T. Jefferson (eds), *Resistance Through Ritual*, London: Routledge.

Mercer, B. (1958) *The Study of Society*, New York: Harcourt-Brace.

Merton, R. (1949) *Social Theory and Social Structure*, New York: Free Press.

Mestrovic, S. (1991) *The Coming Fin de Siecle*, London: Routledge.

Muggleton, D. (1998) 'The post-subculturist', in S. Redhead, D. Wynne and J. O'Connor (eds), *The Clubcultures Reader: Readings in Popular Cultural Studies*, Oxford: Blackwell.

O'Neill, J. (1995) *The Poverty of Postmodernism*, London: Routledge.

O'Neill, J. (1997) 'Parsons's Freud', unpublished lecture, University of Heidelberg, 26-27 June.

Park, R. and Burgess, R. (eds) (1925) *The City*, Chicago: University of Chicago Press.

Parson, T. (1951) *The Social System*, New York: Free Press.

Parsons, T. (1959) 'The school class as a social system: some of its functions in American society', *Harvard Educational Review* XXIX Fall:297-318.

Parsons, T. (1964) *Essays in Sociological Theory*, New York: Free Press.

Parsons, T. (1968) *The Structure of Social Action*, New York: Free Press.

Parsons, T. and White, W. (1961) 'The link between character and society', in S. Lipset and L. Lowenthal (eds) *Culture and Social Character*, New York: Free Press.

Phillipson, M. (1985) *Painting, Language and Metaphor*, London: Routledge.

Redhead, S. (1977) *From Subculture to Clubculture*, Oxford: Blackwell.

Redhead, S., Wynne, D. and O'Conner, J. (eds) (1998) *The Clubcultures Reader: Readings in Popular Cultural Studies*, Oxford: Blackwell.

Saunders, P. (1986) *Social Theory and the Urban Question*, London: Routledge.

Simmel, G. (1902) 'The number of members as determining the sociological form of the group', *The American Journal of Sociology*, 8.

Smith, J. (1995) 'Three images of the visual', in C. Jenks (ed.), *Visual Culture*, London: Routledge.

Sugarman, B. (1967) 'Involvement in youth culture, academic achievement, and conformity in schools', *British Journal of the Sociology of Education*, XVIII (3): 210–22.

Thompson, E.P. (1968) *The Making of the English Working Class*, Harmondsworth: Penguin.

Thompson, E.P. and Yeo, E. (1971) *The Unknown Mayhew*, London: Merlin Press.

Thompson, K. (1982) *Emile Durkheim*, London: BFI Press.

Thornton, S. (1995) *Club Cultures: Music, Media and Subcultural Capital*, Cambridge: Polity.

Thrasher, F. (1927) *The Gang*, Chicago: University of Chicago Press.

Timasheff, N. (1955) *Sociological Theory: Its Nature and Growth*, New York: Random House.

Tolson, A. (1990) 'Social surveillance and subjectification: the emergence of "subculture" in the work of Henry Mayhew', *Cultural Studies*, 4 (2): 97–119.

Tönnies, F. (1887) *Community and Association* (English translation 1955), London: Routledge.

Townsend, P. (1957) *The Family Life of Old People*, London: Routledge.

Turner, G. (1990) *British Cultural Studies*, London: Unwin Hyman.

Urry, J. (2000) *Sociology Beyond Societies*, London: Routledge.

Walkowitz, J. (1992) *City of Dreadful Delight: Narratives of Sexual Danger in Late-Victorian London*, London: Virago.

Weber, M. (1964) *The Theory of Social and Economic Organizations*, New York: Free Press

Whyte, W.F. (1955) *Street Corner Society: The Social Structure of an Italian Slum*, Chicago: University of Chicago Press.

Williams, R. (1963) *Culture and Society 1750–1950*, Harmondsworth: Penguin.

Willis, P. (1977) *Learning to Labour*, Aldershot: Gower.

Wilmott, P. (1966) *Adolescent Boys in East London*, London: Routledge and Kegan Paul.

Wilmott, P. and Wilmott, P. (1963) *The Evolution of Community*, London: Routledge.

Wolfgang, M. and Ferracuti, F. (1967) *The Subculture of Violence: Towards an Integrated Theory in Criminology*, London: Tavistock.

Wright Mills, C. (1943) 'The professional ideology of social pathologists', *American Journal of Sociology*, September, (2): 165–89.

Wright Mills, C. (1959) *The Sociological Imagination*, New York: Oxford University Press.

Wrong, D. (1961) 'The oversocialized conception of man in modern sociology', in Yinger, M. (1960) 'Contraculture and subculture', *American Sociological Review*, 25 (5): 625–635.

Young, K. and Mack, R. (1959) *Sociology and Social Life*, New York: American Book.

Young, M. (1963) *Family and Class in a London Suburb*, London: Routledge.

Young, M. and Wilmott, P. (1957) *Family and Kinship in East London*, London: Routledge.

Zorbaugh, H. (1929) *The Gold Coast and the Slum*, Chicago: University of Chicago Press.

Index